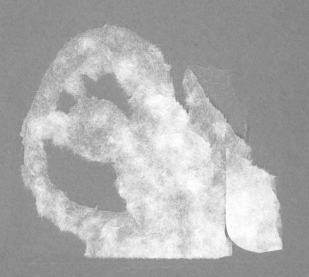

ON THE DECAY OF HUMANISM

W. M. Spackman

RUTGERS UNIVERSITY PRESS

New Brunswick, New Jersey

❋ On the Decay of Humanism

[E S S A Y S]

Copyright © 1967 by Rutgers, The State University
Library of Congress Catalogue Card Number: 66–18876
Manufactured in the United States of America by H. Wolff
Book Manufacturing Co., New York

We wish to thank the publishers listed below for permission to re-print the material indicated.

The Clarendon Press, Oxford: from W. H. D. Rouse, *Demonstrations in Latin Elegiac Verse*, Oxford, 1899.

Holt, Rinehart and Winston, Inc., and The Society of Authors as the literary representative of the Estate of the late A. E. Housman, and Messrs. Jonathan Cape Ltd., publishers of A. E. Housman's *Collected Poems:* from "Oedipus Coloneus" by Sophocles, translated by A. E. Housman, from *The Collected Poems* of A. E. Housman. Copyright 1939, 1940, © 1967 by Holt, Rinehart and Winston, Inc. Reprinted by permission of Holt, Rinehart and Winston, Inc.

The Hudson Review: from Louis Coxe, "Marsh Hawk," reprinted from *The Hudson Review*, Vol. VII, No. 1 (Spring 1954). Copyright 1954 by The Hudson Review, Inc.

Princeton University Press: from Thomas Riggs, "The Progress of Poesy," in *Princeton Verse Between Two Wars*, edited by Allen Tate, Princeton, N.J., 1942.

Random House, Inc., and Faber & Faber: W. H. Auden, "The Song," from his *Homage to Clio*, New York and London, 1960.

ce n'est pas qu'il (c'est moi) sache très bien ce xé
les autres savaient-ils ce xétait que les roses

—Queneau,
Petite Cosmogonie Portative

ACKNOWLEDGEMENTS

It is an especial pleasure to record debts to one's own family. My essay on James owes its structure, a considerable number of its points, and even some of its phrasing, to criticism of the first draft by my son Peter Spackman. My daughter-in-law Nancy Ellsworth Spackman performed a similar humane operation on "Cornbread and Circuses" before its original publication. My daughter Mrs. George M. Hall has let me use a *mot* of hers as epigraph for the Classics essay. And finally, the quotation from the Psalmist in the essay on the *Poetics* is a witty suggestion of my wife's.

I am grateful, too, to my friends of forty years, Alfred Young Fisher and Herman Salinger, for their indulgence in letting me quote from their undergraduate days the poems with which this book ends; and to Fisher, besides, for his critical but benevolent reading of a good deal of the manuscript.

Translations and paraphrases of Greek and Latin quotations are usually my own. But a Classicist would not have to deface his pages with translation if the world were properly run, and I have remedied the mismanagement, when possible, by relegating such things to the notes, out of sight. A few phrases I have left untranslated, even if in Greek, where the sense was clear anyhow; the one exception, the first Greek phrase in the next-to-last paragraph of the *Poetics* essay, can be run down in the *Frogs* of Aristophanes, verse 178.

Parts of "The Learned No," under another title and with a different point, first appeared in *The Classical Journal*, and "Cornbread and Circuses" is a slight re-writing of an article in the *Princeton Alumni Weekly;* I am in the debt of their editors for a courteous *non obstat.*

CONTENTS

ON THE DECAY OF HUMANISM

Topic *sentences*

"Most of the people I write for are dead," said Mr. Auden, "a lot of them hundreds of years ago." This was followed by a short silence.

—Herald Tribune Book Review, 12 February 1956

The lean or big-physics years of the humanities are probably behind us, but recently another form of disquiet, drifting and impalpable as any haze from outer space, has been settling over the assurance with which our universities, for decades now, have been purveying the humane tradition. It is a doubt whether that humane tradition is actually being purveyed. One lectures; but what is heard out there in the murk in front somehow does not always seem to be what one thought one was saying. Recently one undergraduate editor—from the very chair, as it happens, that Edmund Wilson had sat in fifty winters before—brooding on his contemporaries' relation to what they had presumably come to an arts college to find out about, defined the trouble as a complete dislocation of the civilized sensibility: "they reject culture on campus," they "dissociate the culture they study in class from their everyday living." [1] Culture is not the books they excerpt or the art they memorize; what they do take these things to be, God knows, but at any rate not anything that would have made sense in, say, the Renaissance; and the lost ability to re-invest the riches of our cultural heritage might perhaps be stated, in a phrase like the sound of a breath out of the late Mr. Eliot at his most dispirited, as a loss without a sense of loss.

Certainly, if undergraduates fail to become committed to the humane tradition they are exposed to, much of this failure is due to natural immunity. Culture, to one variety of them, is merely the bustle and twitter of erudition; they "reject" it with that verb's full Freudian crudity. To another variety, designed by Heaven to think in tropes anyhow,

Les oeillades du Vrai, le doux rire du Beau

have little to do with it. A painting is a likeness of something; a book is the book's content; *le Vrai* is not a gleam of pretty eyes but a Message; and in short to him

The difference between what's what
And what, regrettably, is not

is going to be culturally undetectable. But there is a third variety (Mr. Wilson's editorial heir is one of them,

4

though an unusually articulate one), and if this variety, too, is unclear about what to his father and his grandfather was perfectly perspicuous, it is fair to conclude that it is not always or only the undergraduate who fails to understand what is being missed, and that there is something false about the professorial approach which has, since the war, been so fashionable as to be professionally obligatory.[2]

The shortest way into my subject, perhaps, is to offer a new—a writer's—construe of that worn passage in the *Apology* about Socrates and the poets. A rich and humorless admirer of Socrates's had insisted (of all possible projects) on asking the Delphic oracle whether anybody anywhere was *sophóteros* than Socrates,[3] and the oracle —which after all had a living to make—had replied No, there wasn't. This amiable nonsense Socrates had used, with a perfectly straight face, as a pious pretext for cross-examining public figures and anybody else on any subject he felt like being a nuisance about. When he got around to the dramatists and poets, Plato has him say

> I would take what struck me as their best-done passages and ask them what they were saying in them; and the embarrassing fact is that I could get a better answer from any random passer-by than from the writers themselves. So I soon saw that it wasn't *sophía* back of their writing, but a sort of native oracular inspiration, as with soothsayers—who turn out beautiful stuff too but can't explain it.

And as we all have a feeling of sentimental attachment for Socrates, we take this at its face value, as if the poets were seriously trying, but failing, to come up with the *explication de texte* that Socrates pretended he was after.

This is hard to believe, the nature of writers being what it is. Let me make Socrates a contemporary of Sophocles, for the sake of the amenities, instead of a generation younger, and then imagine a scene in which he takes up the *Antigone* chorus that begins

πολλὰ τὰ δεινὰ κοὐδὲν ἀν-
θρώπου δεινότερον πέλει

*(Many the wonders I see, but none
See I wonderful more than Man)*

and asks Sophocles, as one celebrity to another, just what did he mean by that adjective δεινός-ή-όν ("wonders"/ "wonderful")? For he'd hardly suppose he meant it as, say, in *Iliad* B 755,

ὅρκου γὰρ δεινοῦ Στυγὸς ὕδατός ἐστιν ἀπορρώξ

". . . for it is a branch of the Styx, water of dire [δεινοῦ] oath." Yet if not that meaning, then what meaning, would he care to say? and so on and so on. Sophocles's good breeding would not have held out long. What has been called [4] "the arrogance of disenchanted insight" would very soon have come into operation, and he would be answering Socrates with the deliberate nonsense that, today too, exasperated genius ends by flinging at the persistent journalist and the dull-witted general public with its interminable "Sir, just what is the place of this poem in your Thought?" and "Now what does *this* line mean?" This is not the kind of angry contempt that Socrates, with his beady eye on the denotative, would be at all likely to comprehend: it would not occur to him that Sophocles might simply see no point in making a serious answer to a man who was not going to see that it *was* serious. Whereas the random passer-by, asked to explain a passage, would assume that some neat explanation had to exist and accordingly find one. Paul Elmer More used to amuse himself by asking random visitors to "explain" Eliot's hippopotamus-poem. They always could.

Thus the fundamental Socratic assumption, that there always is something "there" to impart and explain, remained unimpugned, even unexamined. Plato's mind hardened, and he proceeded to discuss poetry as if it were a form of instruction, undeterred by the silliness of the logical consequences this involved him in.[5] And so here we are today—the writer is still a vatic imparter of portents, shambling along draped in all the trappings of theomantic and chrismatory pomp; and if he can't always "explain" what he's telling us, there are massed regiments of academic minds who can. And do.

In our time, from various accidents of fashion and personality, the basic disagreement—for everyone but the narrowest of philosophers—is whether literature is something a writer writes or the synthesis of signs the establishment tends to deal in instead: is Sophocles the answer or is Socrates? For years now, college students have been told, "Socrates." Yet if this answer has not been conveying what it was devised to convey, then perhaps it is time we tried telling them "Sophocles" instead; and in the essays that follow I have tried to do just that—I have looked at five specific literary phenomena with no professional *parti pris* but a writer's. For from a writer's standpoint, the trouble is plain. The creative artist or writer is one thing, his interpreter the professor another, with a different habit of mind altogether; and the interpreter misinterprets. Or perhaps the more articulate your professor, the likelier he is to deal with a work of art less in its own terms than as a mere starting point for whatever he has thought up to say instead.

Nor, for at least three reasons, does he notice what he is doing wrong. First, he makes no real attempt to understand how a work of art comes about, how it is *made* (in both senses), how in a word the creative intelligence operates—or indeed what kind of intelligence it is to be seen as. Next, he fails to perform first of all the act of aesthetic estimation which for the creative temperament is *always* first; and so, lacking any primary perception of what makes a defect a defect or beauties beauties, he is likely to be unable even to tell you which is which. This is easiest to observe in academic judgment of contemporary writers like Cary, Faulkner, or Hemingway, where the comforting consensus of time has still to offer its substitute assessment. And lastly, he keeps seeing Meanings where none are, ignoring the kind of meaning that *is* there, and discovering in the creative mind all sorts of characteristics that, creatively speaking, are nonsense.

Now Plato no doubt used the phrase that I have rendered "a sort of native oracular inspiration" because it does loosely distinguish poetic statement from how the

mind works in setting down straightforward information and the like in prose; but it is not a good description of how the creative mind actually operates. For one
thing, φύσει τινί ("by a kind of natural bent") begs the
question in one way, and ἐνθουσιάζοντες ("being *entheos,*
full of the god") begs it in another. But worse, it is a
description that misdescribes, for it makes the writer
a mere voice, without the power to revise and rearrange
the phrases it utters, or the art to polish them—little
more in fact than a kind of wind-tunnel from which
issue the blustery and over-stylized admonitions of a
pedagogical Heaven.

What does take place is altogether different. Writing
is a process of choosing and changing, a rearrangement,
among phrases obtruded through into the consciousness
from the endless mumbling singsong babble of the in-
nermost whatever-it-is, a kind of seething of molten
sound that any sentence anybody utters is the ultimate
petrifaction of. What makes the writer a writer is, first,
that his material is unusually rich—there is

flung up momently the sacred river—

and secondly, that he knows how to make it a great deal
richer still by manipulating it. It is *these* factors that
set the writer as far apart from the passer-by as Plato
makes him seem to be. But it is *only* this that sets him
apart: in every other way he merely shares with the rest
of us the under-rewarded and unprepossessing lot of
man, and is as full of illusions, as fatuous, as prone to
folly, as likely to be as disastrously dead wrong, as any-

9

one else. To suppose that one can be improved or instructed from such a source is as preposterous an expectation as Chaerephon's in consulting the oracle about Socrates and *sophia* in the first place.

2

For, fluency aside, what is an actual writer like?

To start with, he rarely has more to recommend him than any other human being; perhaps less, for his egotism is usually unpleasant. Milton was an impossible person, Proust and Joyce almost unimaginable. At bottom, no doubt, is the irresponsibility of the eccentric. The ranting escapes of English literary men to the *mezzogiorno,* for instance, are as symbolic a phenomenon as they are historically a constant: the real difference between Lawrence, Joyce, and Graves in this century, and Byron and Shelley in the nineteenth, is neither spiritual nor intellectual but simply pecuniary—the Romantic aristocracy could at least afford their own behavior. At one end of the scale eccentricity shows up as madness, and there is always a certifiable percentage in the official literary canon; suicides, moreover, like Mrs. Woolf, Hart Crane, and Hemingway, are frequent. But mere working survival is no criterion; imagine a *sane* man's going through the self-inflicted hell that Tolstoi describes in that disguised fragment of autobiography, *The Death of Ivan Ilych!* Nor at the other end of the scale is the sheer lack of practical wisdom much less astonishing. A great poet like Pope expended half the energy of a lifetime polishing and elaborating that mere "paper of a day," the *Dunciad.* A great poet *manqué,* Plato, reached the conclusion that literature, which is concerned with imagining the real world, should be suppressed altogether if it did not concern itself with the world *he* imagined was real.

Moreover, writers often *know* surprisingly little. Sometimes the reason is innocence. Miss Austen's earlier novels show only a preliminary, almost a girlish, notion of male character: one has only to set Mr. Darcy beside one of his equivalents in Miss Compton-Burnett to be startled by the difference in penetration. Nor is it, with Miss Austen, the customary difficulty of ambivalence that a woman novelist's ego smoulders over in constructing a hero, but rather that her eye keeps lingering on the trappings, her attention seduced. Sometimes, again, a writer's ignorance looks like a consequence of some hidden distaste for his subject. One is no more likely to find out what a woman is like from Faulkner than from John O'Hara: each simply libels woman as frigidly, sex for sex, and with as empty a heart, as, say, Miss McCarthy libels man.[6] Or still again, it may be that narcissism cripples or stunts a writer's ability to see what he looks at for what it is. Hemingway for example ended up mistaking knowingness for knowledge, with a sort of sports-columnist's pedantry about very specialized detail in a highly restricted field.[7] His real topic was fear; but beyond this he gives the impression of knowing really very little about a great deal, most of his later fiction showing so little knowledge of the world that it is embarrassing to read. Even the Fitzgerald he sneered at knew more.

Now the writer feels he can permit himself all this, and indeed anything else, because he has a gift that sets him so far above the *hypocrite lecteur* that he doesn't look like a *semblable* or a *frère* at all. For the writer possesses

that one talent which is death to hide,

and while he has no intention of hiding it, the plain fact is that he could not: the underground river of phrases welling inexhaustibly up is a natural phenomenon and uncontrollable. It is however likely to be perfectly irrelevant, a good part of the time, to whatever the writer happens to be actually at work on. A novelist of my acquaintance once indulged me by compiling a sort of anthology of the incidental nonsense that intruded upon his concentration. There were parodies in quantity, all the way from Lamartine (*Un seul hêtre vous manque, et tout est déboisé*) and Irving Berlin (A pretty girl is like an allergy) to such stylistic pastiches as

No sooner God's command was given:
SWIVE—*than behold, the boy had swiven.*

There was a profusion of tawdry dialogue-gags ("Some time you must tell me where you buy your friends"), a lot of sheer noise (*Ma mie, mes mots muent*—which he translated "Darling, my epigrams are moulting"), a title for his autobiography (Down Wind from Father), and at least one beautiful pentameter,

Or the soul, trembling in its case of air.

Perhaps most typical was what looks like the close of a Gautier quatrain which he found his mind reciting when he awoke one morning:

No shimming or disaster shakes
The swart profusions of our sin.

Such things are the soul's true surrealism. Not one of them was anything he could possibly make use of. And although he has trouble finding names for his actual characters, he was flooded with nonsensical suggestions —a hired man called Bashed-in Johnson, Indians with names like Mary Buxom Horse, and an Eskimo avant-garde composer, Mildred Whalesmile.

The best a writer can do with this endless seething of sound is echo that modest line in *Les Mariés de la Tour Eiffel,*

Puisque ces mystères me dépassent, feignons d'en être
l'organisateur.

Cocteau is exact: even the finished work has often to be refinished, and then refinished again, one's organization having been an illusion too, and out of one's hands. This is another among the many facets of creativity that Socrates did not see: he was too busy insisting that art have some sort of Socratic significance to bother with actual artistic fact, and my general point throughout this book will be that his heirs, the professorate, never really look at what they are discussing either. Like their single-minded great exemplar, they simply convert into their own terms.

Now what one ought to see, instead, is that, though *la folle du logis* is the source of literature, it is the *organisateur* that, as best it can, shapes it.

Something of the division of labor involved can perhaps be seen in a tour de force of Auden's:

> *So large a morning so itself to lean*
> *Over so many and such little hills*
> *All at rest in roundness and rigs of green*
> *Can cope with a rebellious wing that wills*
> *To better its obedient double quite*
> *As daring in the lap of any lake*
> *The wind from which ascension puts to flight*
> *Tribes of a beauty that no care can break.*
>
> *Climbing to song it hopes to make amends*
> *For whiteness drabbed for glory said away*
> *And be immortal after but because*
> *Light upon a valley where its love was*
> *So lacks all picture of reproach it ends*
> *Denying what it started up to say.*

This is a marvel as much because Auden is one of the greatest technical masters that ever lived as because he is a "great poet." Parts of this sonnet are typical of "unconscious" production, like that Elizabethan

> *For whiteness drabbed for glory said away*

—though it may not have presented itself first in just those words (and may even have been salvaged from a notebook). The technique consists in creating, to sandwich it, two lines that give the illusion of being up to it. The opening of the octave, also, has the meaninglessness and beauty of pure sound characteristic of unconscious creation; but then, just as line 2 begins to peter out, comes the prosodic legerdemain of line 3, lifting up and saving everything. Finally, there is the dazzling decision to make octave and sestet each a single unpunctuated sentence. There is nobody else who can *do* this sort of thing; and that, in passing, was also, I hope, one of Auden's reasons for writing it.

Now, a man who can turn out such a poem is so unimaginably more articulate (if nothing more) than the man in the street that they hardly do seem to belong to the same species. There is, besides, to add to the illusion, the whole staggering difference between their outlooks: to the man in the street this sonnet is of such a black obscurity that he isn't even likely to find his way through the subordinate clauses. And it *is* obscure in the sense of having no demonstrable meaning beyond itself. It is largely due to such differences that the vaticine misinterpretation which the *Apology* puts in Socrates's mouth is perpetuated from one generation to the next. One has only to listen, surely, to perceive that the great writer is *not* quite of the same species as the rest of us, but *éntheos* or whatever adjective is fashionable at the time, and accordingly σοφώτερος ἢ κατ' ἄνθρωπον—with more than human *sophía*.

So much for the writer and how he operates, and for the background of professorial misconstructions. Now for the strange forms that this takes.

3

Il est bon quelquefois de s'aveugler soi-même,
Et bien souvent l'erreur est le bonheur suprême,

says Lisette in Destouches's *Le Glorieux;* and supreme happiness, to the orthodox academic mind today, is a roll in the catnip of semantics. The writer, for the professor of literature, is always "saying" something, and the more sophisticated the professor, the more this something becomes a System, a Whole. It normally does not occur to him that what a writer is makes it unlikely that what he says will be any less trivial than what the rest of us say. It will just be infinitely *better* said. But that is not the same, in terms of ultimate truth or other irrelevances, as being more worth saying.

For the fundamental academic error is the persistent equation of meaning with formal meaning, informational meaning, something that to the writer is likely to be of altogether secondary importance. Any old jargon can convey its *what;* the born writer works at the ineffable *how.* If Auden's sonnet were translated somehow into a version that the random passer-by understood, it would evidently no longer be Auden's sonnet. But this is not just because the words would be different. The point is that it is not even translatable, for (a) it was not written as that *kind* of communication, and (b) it has, as message, only itself to convey anyhow. It is not a statement but a style. And since what one has to look for in a piece of writing is what the writer actually put there ("style"), the professorial eye is looking for—and therefore finding—the wrong thing entirely. Looking for the wrong thing is even exalted into basic axiom: a whole system of academic approach is blurted out in a letter to *The Times Literary Supplement* [8] that speaks of "aspects of Euripides's art which the great dramatist himself was unaware of." There are reasons—I shall suggest some in a moment—for the persistence of academic error. But persist it does; and in effect the standard college lecture on literature has become an act of translating, to the general befuddlement, things that have to be read *in* the language they were written in if they are to be understood at all.

Not keeping one's eye on the fundamental of style has two immediate consequences. There is, first, the ludicrous one that professors never lecture on *bad* writing: semantically there is simply no way of recognizing it. One could audit every literature course in pretty much every college in the country and never suspect that any writer in the canon, major or minor, had ever written a line that fell much short of the masterly. *Paradise Regained* may not be quite up to *Paradise Lost*—but it's all Milton, isn't it? Henry James's reputation, as I shall show in the next essay, is a formidable example of this stone-blindness of the sensibilities. Wordsworth's is another: we are told that, for example,

> *Waters on a starry night*
> *Are beautiful and fair*

is a poetic miracle—when all that could make one think so is that in comparison with most of Wordsworth it *is* a poetic miracle.

The second critical mishap when one fails to concentrate on style is that one's judgment, musing on content instead, will almost certainly confuse what a writer says with what he says it about—a novel with the events it narrates—and so end up issuing mere ethical pronouncements about the misconduct of fictional personages or the nobilities of a story-line. This is all the more plausible for being Aristotelian; how else, moreover, is one to award or withhold that sagacious adjective "great"?

Even an educated taste may be an inadequate safeguard: one of the best-balanced recent books on the novel [9] grades *Les Liaisons Dangereuses* below *La Princesse de Clèves* because the people and events it deals in are (though this is not how it puts it) ignobler. Unhappily, discussion of content is standard procedure for the average professor: citing, as he must, works in languages he cannot himself understand, and uneasily conscious that what he is reading is not Homer or Tolstoi but Mr. Graves or Mrs. Garnett, he is naturally as brief on style as is decent, and so the content becomes in effect the major matter of criticism.

Now a number of excuses can be put forward for the aesthetic deficiencies of the academic mind. The chief trouble is of course that there are never anything like enough good natural critics to go round, that is, not enough people who can actually tell good work from run-of-the-mill. But aside from this, professors are the entailed heirs of older professors who had little native or educated taste either, and who were also nearer in time to such stultifying forces as Victorian vulgarity and a German doctorate taken *in situ*. Many, again, have little real interest in literature as literature anyhow: their heart's love has been given to erudition, and a campus is a refuge where they can nestle with it and be alone. Many who do love literature are first entrapped and then slowly suffocated by academic conventions as to what, at a given period, criticism can fashionably or even profitably be about. For years a highly approved field has been the criticism of contemporary poetry; as practically all of this is neither good nor bad, or indeed much of anything but more of the same, a man's judgment grows dull from apathy and mere disuse. It is easy enough to tell a good epic from a bad, but discriminating among not-really-good and really-not-bad minor short lyrics in a not-really-very-lyric-anyway era is beyond the powers of nearly anybody. The academic world ought to reflect on a couple of sentences by one of its few real critics: "*All* the ambitious poetry of the last six hundred years is less 'original' than any but a few of its readers ever realize. . . . A difficulty is that modern critics spend much of their time in the perusal of writing that really is more or less original, and negligible." [10] And finally, whether a professor likes or doesn't like literature, he cannot afford to make a practice of calling any of it dull, or trash: if an author isn't well worth reading, then how is one going to justify learned papers or a dissertation on him?

To avoid having to think about such professional dilemmas as these, the academic establishment has devised several ways of talking about literature without having first to say whether literature is what it in fact is, or what makes it so. The most ingenious of these devices, as I have said, is talking about its Meanings instead. Meaning masks everything: it does not say that a writer is "good" or "bad"; for that matter it does not tell you whether he is even a writer; it simply makes him unassailably portentous. As early as the 1930's, the shrewder professors had seen that they could produce a more flowery and articulate, indeed a far happier, effect by treating literature less as what it was than as what it stood for. This critical method has become by now so highly articulate that it hardly needs literature except as *point de repère* or pretext: you can simply replace any work under discussion with what you describe it as. This has prospered wonderfully: the manufacture of English-department *boulle* for example is a self-sufficient industry. One may argue whether the late Mr. Blackmur's brilliance did his colleagues a disservice by setting them a standard beyond their reach, but the chinoiseries of imitation mandarins leave little doubt what the standard was.

Or again, the philosophers come soliloquizing in, and the literature vanishes in the meaning altogether. Here, the infestations of extravaganza are as various as the self-deceptions of man; the sonorous analyses of what may or may not be there are unabashed. At one end of the scale is what one might call literary pietism, a method based on the hagiolatrous invocation of Yeats, Dante, and Eliot, no matter what the topic, somewhat as in the tenth century one took the Holy Ghost as premise, or as Marxist pietists today invoke the Dialectic. At the low-church end there is always some new sub-Hegelian aesthetics or other to fiddle with, in lofty disregard of

the simple act of creation. How does one write a poem?
Listen:

> the primary requirement of poetry, which is the ob-
> scure knowing, by the poet, of his own subjectivity, is
> inseparable from, is one with another requirement—
> the grasping, by the poet, of the objective reality of the
> outer and inner world: not by means of concepts and
> conceptual knowledge, but by means of an obscure
> knowledge which I shall describe in a moment as
> knowledge through affective union.[11]

Well, *"nous n'avons point chez nous de poètes de la
connaissance"*—that is not how Valéry [12] meant it, but it
will serve. The methods of philosophy are the more
damaging in that they give non-philosophers the illusion
of saying something profound two or three times a page;
and this in turn induces the still fonder notion that profundity is what it is all about anyhow. A philosopher's
definitions rarely have much to do with how a writer
writes; they do not even explain why anyone would
think they did. An impatient commentator might indeed sum the whole methodology up by paraphrasing an
epigram of Rivarol's: *c'est un terrible avantage que de
n'avoir rien compris, mais il ne faut pas en abuser.*

Our large urban universities have moreover imported
from France, or at any rate from Paris, a specialized
form of the confusion of writing with speculation, a
form based in the French habit of not really distinguish-
ing between writers and *intellectuels*. In France, this is
venial enough: the standard French man of letters, Sartre for instance, is after all as much generalized intel-

lectual as writer, and in Paris the university is right over there in the fifth arrondissement. So it is natural that

> la pensée abstraite, jadis admis dans le Vers même, étant devenue presque impossible à combiner avec les émotions immédiates que l'on souhaitait de provoquer à chaque instant . . . se soit transportée dans la phase de préparation et dans la théorie du poème. La philosophie, et même la morale, tendirent à fuir les oeuvres pour se placer dans les réflexions qui les précèdent.[13]

The French believe themselves to be *lucides;* I imagine, rightly. But they have never quite noticed that this belief does not actually make for clarity of mind. It has given them an advanced and much admired critical vocabulary, yes; their intellectually fashionable writers are wonderful at living up to it, and at preserving and enriching its special irrelevances. But we are wanting in such things; and in our native destitution therefore we can observe how firmly *le bon Dieu* has made in French literature the distinction French criticism affects not to see. I need cite only André Breton. There have been few *intellectuels* more modish or more vociferous, yet when he really writes—things like his dazzling *Ma femme à la chevelure de feu de bois*—he differs only stylistically, not in the happy naïveté of what he is doing, from Gautier's

> Que tu me plais dans cette robe
> Qui te déshabille si bien,
> Faisant jaillir ta gorge en globe,
> Montrant tout nu ton bras païen.

The triviality is open and complete, and, like Pascal, *on est étonné et ravi, car on s'attendait de voir un auteur, et on trouve un homme.*[14]

Finally, our academic critics have found that they can profitably become biographers instead, historians, and go sifting through the dumps of earlier learned guesses and doctoral insights that mark a distinguished tomb. Considerations of the circumstances of a given work's composition are, naturally, not a serious basis for criticism of its qualities as literature. But erudition is still erudition: *grammatici certant* because otherwise they would be without occupation. And so all about us are stacked the sterile archives of *Homo Hypostatéos,* or Every Man His Own Doctorate. One simply latches onto an unutilized author and becomes the authority on him. If there is an authority already, one can become an authority on selected aspects; or if one is smarter, oust the authority *en titre.* One can even fasten upon an author who has never crossed anybody's mind as worth becoming an authority on. The insight-scalpel, today, is within the reach of the lowliest graduate student; all that is needed is a stiff.

Such, alas, to a writer, is the usual aspect of the academic mind. Small wonder that its efforts at interpreting him leave him aghast. *"Que dire à ces gens qui, croyant posséder une clef, n'ont de cesse qu'ils aient disposé votre oeuvre en forme de serrure?"* [15] Plato himself could hardly do worse.

What remedies, then, what sort of mended curriculum, can the disabused mind propose? What specific things besides the abjuring of ingenuity can one reasonably require the academic establishment to undertake to do?

First—first by far—would be the extirpation of Meaning from the literary course, and a study of style and form implanted in its place.[16] For without style (and what could be more obvious?) there *is* no art or literature; and to overstate the corollary for emphasis, plastic art is wholly, and literature almost wholly, style. What they "say" is for the most part perfectly irrelevant in terms of what they above all are. Consider two versions of an identical meaning, the μὴ φῦναι chorus in the *Oedipus at Colonus:*

> *Far best were ne'er to be;*
> *But, having seen the day,*
> *Next best by far for each to flee*
> *As swiftly as each may . . .*

This is Lewis Campbell, and not literature; for that matter not really English. Now here is Housman:

> *Thy portion esteem I highest,*
> *Who wast not ever begot;*
> *Thine next, being born who diest*
> *And straightway again art not.*

The style is everything. One can even produce versions that are word for word the same, yet one flat and the other respectably literate, for example, Propertius 1, 1, 7:

Et mihi iam toto furor hic non deficit anno,

which means

And this madness has not left me for a whole year now

but which should be translated, Pound having shown the way,

And now for a whole year this madness has not left me.

All that is wanted is an attention to style—and automatically the undergraduate would begin to learn a valuable truth that had never crossed his mind: how *bad* most writing is.

A revised curriculum would also deal in as much detail with a writer's natural limits as with what are purveyed, never terribly convincingly, as his predecessors or other "influences." One seldom hears academic people talk as if they noticed what the writer *fundamentally* does with that infinity of material, man. For above all what he does is *leave out.* His praetermissions are of course sometimes determined by the form, or by a convention: epic and tragedy, for instance, omit the common people. But in the main it is a matter of native bent: even the greatest, the "universal," writers work each within the home domain of his disposition, with its private topography and vistas and its selected fauna. Experiences beyond his boundary lines are beyond him in another sense also—he can't handle them, or they bore him, or he doesn't suspect their existence, or he excludes them programmatically, or he'll get around to them when he damn' well gets around to 'em. Or some dreary incompetent's done 'em already. Homer has no serious theology; Dante, such mazes of it that for all we know the Creator Himself is delighted to have our professorial footnotes explaining things. Or again, who in antiquity beyond Euripides, Aristophanes, and Ovid really wrote about what has since antiquity been our major topic, woman?

Now part of the duty of the critic here is to decide when such limitations as these are due to the contours of a given writer's temperament and when to his native incapacity. For example Vergil's Dido is a Hellenistic trope and Mr. Sutherland's wit has deflated Aeneas: the *Aeneid* is "an adventure story of which the hero does not like adventure." [17] We read Vergil for other things entirely, putting up with his aesthete's character-drawing by the same convention that lets us accept, say, a travertine Galatea as representing an armful of warm girl. Or again, Joyce did not write tragedy: his equivalent is a kind of keening pathos, the mumble and misery of small-tradespeople ("I done me best when I was let"), and even those occasions when *mentem mortalia tangunt* occur chiefly in his early work. The undergraduate must be made to argue whether, in so splendid a genius, this is a flaw or a mode of development. He must investigate what went wrong with the endings of *La Princesse de Clèves* and *Zazie dans le Métro,* or of a given novel of Mme. de Vilmorin's. I can even conceive of a fascinating (though exhausting) course devoted to something like rewriting the first ball in *Pride and Prejudice* in the manners of, in turn, Djuna Barnes, Elizabeth Bowen, and Ivy Compton-Burnett. The undergraduate who survived such a course would never again be in doubt about the facts of literature.

Finally, for those interminable lectures on the creative artist's Thought there should be substituted straightforward investigations of the defects and eccentricities of temperament that I described earlier, and their erratic consequences for a given body of work. There is much deliberate artistic obfuscation: as my hypothetical Sophocles might have said of Socrates, Claims he can't understand what I write, does he, the πανοῦργος? by god I'll give him an explanation he'll understand even less. A lot of work, too, is *voulu* rather than written. Avant-garde groups for example tend to be composed of two or three genuine and original talents plus a cloud of hangers-on who have, at best, merely a knack or a longing; and since the smaller the talent the greater the need for theory as justification, the bulk of avant-garde work is produced to illustrate, and conform to, whatever program the program happens to be. Aesthetically such work is negligible: being in a sense a game, a demonstration, it is zero as anything else. It has even been argued, by the malicious, that a fundamental axiom of avant-garde writing is that no intelligent reader should expect to derive anything as trivial as pleasure from reading it.[18]

Again, the lazy-mindedness of the artist has to be set

before the undergraduate in terms of its consequences. The typical first novel is a handy paradigm. It tends to be naturally gloomy and emotionally out of balance—

Sto sospirando o lagrimando vado

and so forth—since a still adolescent "Unconscious" is running the show and the writer himself is too inexperienced to countervail. Second novels are noticeably different *if* the writer is artist enough to see that every new book calls for a new form, and perhaps style, as much as for a new topic. But the first novel, as things stand, will have been kindly treated by reviewers; and the average writer uses this factitious encouragement as an excuse for making his second novel a lazy (sometimes, a nervous) copy of his first; its style becomes, in his mind, not the tentative thing it in fact was but felicitous and definitive, and his; and having soon become habit, it continues to disfigure his work to the end of his days with the forms and mannerisms of intellectual infancy.

Writers even avoid work by borrowing other writers' clichés. *Sanctuary* for instance demonstrated that a touch of disemboweling and other preposterous forms of violence could be made to give the impression of a novel bursting with life, and the Southern novel has been standardized ever since: the generation of Garrett seems to clasp the blueprint as gratefully as did the generation of Warren. The standard Jewish novel has become an equal cliché, and is now as predictable as the dreary labor novels of the 1930's or those standardized French recitations on the French bourgeoisie. We are even working our way toward a standardized fairy—and all this writer's rubbish too must find its place among the grim particulars of reform.

Whether any such process of uncomfortable betterment is at all likely to come about is another matter. *On ne se dit jamais bien nettement qu'on n'est pas aimée,* said Mme. de Tencin; and the academic mind is no more capable than anybody else's would be of seeing what it does as other than what it thinks it is doing. *Quisque suos patimur manes,* nor would Socrates have conceived that I was serious.

NOTES

1. *Princeton Alumni Weekly,* 25 January 1966, p. 6. The inability to handle cultural realities extends to what a generation ago would have been commonplaces: undergraduates even "tend to confuse creative writers with political radicals"!

2. Uneasiness about the critical/pedagogical fashion has been in the air for some time, a sober statement of it being Richard Foster, *The New Romantics* (Bloomington, 1962), p. 196: "Among the New Critics, only Cleanth Brooks comes to mind—and perhaps also Empson—as engaged mainly in the detailed and selfless analysis of particular works of literature. . . . we have mostly general or 'speculative' essays from the critics [who] even when they begin with a text or a corpus of texts, will tend to move away toward general considerations of the imagination, the modern world, the nature of poetry, even the nature of reality."

Abroad, the dissatisfaction has just burst out in full-scale critical war, Raymond Picard's witty and sardonic *Nouvelle Critique ou Nouvelle Imposture* (Paris, 1965) having now been answered (not very convincingly) by Roland Barthes in a pamphlet *Critique et Vérité* (Paris, 1966); a more detailed and "philosophized" answer is Serge Doubrovsky's *Pourquoi la Nouvelle Critique* (Paris, 1966), though unfortunately his preface then proceeds to oversimplify things again in order to give Barthes a *coup de main.* The dispute is of course along specialized French lines; but Picard's charge that the new critics show *"une étrange indifférence, dans la littérature, à ce qui est littéraire"* (p. 104) is merely another way of saying what Foster says above, and the technique of overburdening a text

with speculative commentary appears constantly in Barthes, e.g.,
his saying of the critic, *"S'il lit*
    La fille de Minos et de Pasiphaé,
son rôle n'est pas d'établir qu'il s'agit de Phèdre (les philologues le
feront très bien), mais de concevoir un réseau de sens tel qu'y pren-
nent place, selon certaines exigences logiques . . . le thème
chthonien et le thème solaire" (p. 64).

    On either side of the Atlantic, it seems to be an ancestral longing
for synthesis, for Answers, *"la nostalgie de l'Unité perdue"* (Doubrovsky, p. 89) that causes a good deal of the trouble: cf. Erich
Auerbach, *Literary Language and Its Public* (London, 1965), pp. 16
ff., for a wry statement of the dilemma.

3. "Abler," "more knowledgeable," "more gifted intellectually." The
noun *sophia* connotes political shrewdness, or a workman's skill, or
sound judgment, as much as it does "wisdom." *Philosophia* similarly means a habit of inquiry, scientific investigation, and so on;
"love of wisdom" is a freshman translation.

4. In *The Times Literary Supplement,* 29 April 1965, p. 321.

5. The sheer wrong-headedness of *Republic,* Book X, must be hard
even for Platonists to accept. Homer for example isn't up to Ly-
curgus in law-making (599d) or to Thales in practical science (600a)
or to Pythagoras in teaching a way of life (600b); Homer and Hesiod
weren't "able to make men better" and hence nobody employed
them (600d); in fact all the arts are useless, being concerned with
something "far from the truth," elegance of finish (603b); drama is
bad for us because it portrays violence instead of law and order
(604a—though his examples are not the *logos* and *nomos* he pre-
tends they are but merely *éthos* or even *schema,* upperclass-Athe-
nian deportment); and in short "no poetry but hymns and odes
about good men is to be tolerated in our state" (607a), for art does
not "lay hold of truth" (608a).

    "You know as well as I do," says Socrates (601b), "what poor stuff
poets' work turns out to be once you've stripped off the stylistic
embellishments and got down to what it actually says"; and this
childish cake-and-icing view of literature might be taken to excuse
Plato's nonsense. But Plato was a writer himself; to abuse writers
and the way they operate, when he himself operated that way, is as
tiresome a piece of hypocrisy as the history of criticism is ever likely
to show. The cost of ambivalence is moreover high: nearly all
Plato's work has flaws of proportion, sometimes gross ones—imagine
inserting a *detailed* discussion of immortality in the grave beauty of
the *Phaedo.*

6. Faulkner is not alone in being ungallant just where the myth leads
us to expect the very posturing quintessence of courtliness—*all*
Southern writers seem to have it in for Southern womanhood.
(What *does* go on down there?)

    As it happens, the real job on the lady was done long ago by a

Continentalized Englishman, "Stephen Hudson," in *Elinor Col-house,* a minor masterpiece of characterization despite its cliché prose (and despite the mediocrity of the rest of *A True Story* and the sheer grotesque badness of *The Other Side*).

7. This seems to me a fairer explanation than abusing him for his self-exploitation and "his cagey little self-advertising mind" (Virgil Thomson in *The Paris Review,* #33, p. 164; cf. the anonymous "Our Poppa which art in Havana, Hollywood be thine aim"). The creative artist must not be reproached for having a sound mercantile sense too: how often has not Picasso, to the general applause, turned Picasso-factory.

8. 27 August 1964.

9. Martin Turnell, *The Novel in France* (New York, 1958).

10. John Berryman, in *Partisan Review,* April 1949, p. 383.

    One recalls the fretful sentence that Byron set down in his journal, 6 December 1813: "It is odd that when I do read, I can bear only the chicken broth of—*any* thing but Novels."

11. Jacques Maritain, *Creative Intuition and Poetic Knowledge* (New York, 1955), p. 83.

12. Paul Valéry, *Variété* (Paris, 1924), p. 117.

13. *Ibid.,* p. 100.

14. *Pensées,* I, 29.

15. "Julien Gracq," in the *Mercure de France,* June 1964, p. 219.

    Happy exceptions to the standard professorial epideictics do of course appear: Edward Stokes wrote *The Novels of Henry Green* (London, 1959) while Senior Lecturer in English at the University of Tasmania, and Charles Burkhart his equally admirable *I. Compton-Burnett* (London, 1965) at Temple. Each man has his mind fully on the writing before him, not on some critical ὄγκος thought up for the occasion; neither book is an expanded dissertation.

16. The ultimate in meaning-gimmicks is probably the *Syntopicon,* in which literature is nothing *but* the store-house of "ideas." I take it as read that Dwight Macdonald has exposed the nonsense of this once for all in his *New Yorker* piece reprinted in *Against the American Grain* (New York, 1962), pp. 242 sqq.

17. Donald Sutherland, in a paper read to the Colorado Education Association, 28 October 1949.

18. Of course fashions in boring change. James and Meredith verbigerated; Henry Miller, ditto plus excreta; Faulkner perfected boredom by po'-white rant, Southerners being naturally garrulous anyhow; Beckett has superstitiously exorcized, presumably as sin, the brilliance of *Murphy.*

James, James

So much for the general tone of realism; and this
being granted, it is of little moment that the rustics
use genitives in *-oio* and epic aorists, and do not
elide all their vowels.

—R. J. Cholmeley,
The Idylls of Theocritus

The English have never taken much of a part in the
Henry James discussion; but in 1928 Herbert Read, in
his *English Prose Style,* set down in peroration a paragraph that, both in what it said and in what it was blind
to, might stand as epigraph for almost anything American Jamesists have written since. Sir Herbert (as he now
is) took as his culminating stylists Newman and James;
and James, he wrote,

> developed a very complex and a very personal style, a
> style which has encountered a good deal of shallow de-
> preciation. But, once his mind was made up, the aim
> of Henry James was essentially the same as Newman's

—to explain clearly and exactly his meaning, and not to bother about writing for writing's sake. Now the 'meaning' which Henry James was concerned to express was generally very complicated. It was concerned with life at its finest creative point—the point where moral judgments are formed. The deeper this penetrating mind delved into the psychological complexity of human motives the more involved his world became. But it was obviously the real world, the only world worth considering, once your course is set that way. Henry James went ahead, fearlessly, irretrievably, into regions where few are found who care to follow him.[1]

The largely rhetorical intent of this last sentence is betrayed by its inelegance: Sir Herbert did not mean that one could follow James into this amiable region if one were there already. But there is more than this to clear away before seeing just what it is that Sir Herbert was talking his way around. For example, not just Newman or James but every writer tries to set down his meaning in the way he means it: this is simply what writing is. Again, as to James's complexities, the sophisticated critic today has a less undisabused notion of the subtle: to a man of Mr. Sutherland's range, "the analyses [in] James and Proust which once seemed infinitely delicate now appear broad and burly enough." [2] Still again, that "life at its finest creative point—the point where moral judgments are formed" looks very like an aesthetic *petitio principii*. And so on.

What then remains is a kind of oblique formulation of two real difficulties. The first has engaged American academic critics, though with little profit, for two or three decades: if James's world is "obviously the real world," why do we not feel this to be obvious immediately, without so much critical fine language assembled in proof? And second (though Sir Herbert no doubt felt his book as a whole had dealt with this one): does bothering about writing for writing's sake, as he puts it, somehow involve being imprecise and unclear?

Now, what seems to have happened to the first of these difficulties since James's centenary is that it has hardened into a kind of dilemma, and this in turn has constrained nearly everyone to discover ways out. The late F. O. Matthiessen had James's real world stay real but cut its size down: James, he suggested, "saw only limited parts of the human comedy," with a number of "qualities of our ordinary life quite missing." [3] This however is true of anybody from Homer on; it has perhaps only the merit of looking very like that delimitation of James's own in Chapter 20 of *The Golden Bowl*, "the convenience of a society so placed that it had only its own sensibility to consider." Mr. Edel rejects any such limiting of intention: "Not only did [James] seek to make the novel convey reality, but he set himself to discovering the best techniques by which verisimilitude might be attained." [4] On the other horn of the dilemma (if that is what it is) stands Mr. Blackmur's equally categorical "we believe in [James's novels] only as we believe in hellish or heavenly fables," [5] the real world banished altogether. Mr. Wilson and Mr. Sutherland are perhaps alone in not evading or being made uneasy by what they see, the one with his "ambiguity," the other with a redefinition of James's later work as disinterested as it is suave, "a continuum less of events than of considerations of their meaning." [6]

What then *is* this opacity of disquiet that hangs like an intellectual haze over so illustrious a literary tomb? Is it something in James's work itself? Or is it, rather, in the minds of his critics?—who, having read Mr. Blackmur's "There has never been a body of work so eminently suited to criticism," [7] mistook this for an invitation to perform. Or is neither of these things a cause, and ought we instead seek an explanation among the routine self-deceptions of critical eloquence, like Mr. Leavis's phrase "the profound seriousness of his [James's] interest in life"? [8] This is the weighty and accepted way to talk about James, but it merely misleads us (and Mr. Leavis) twice: it says nothing about James that cannot be said of hundreds of writers (i.e., it is meaningless), and it completely dissembles James's overmastering interest, which was his craft. To turn against Mr. Leavis a sentence of his own, "What [he] doesn't appear to recognize sufficiently is that a preoccupation with [life] wouldn't necessarily be identifiable with the novelist's true creative preoccupation." [9] Nor do we find the longed-for perspicuity even in poetic guidance: Mr. Auden's poem about James is not about James.

What we have to explain is how on one page Sir Herbert's real world can be "imitated" with every circumstance and fidelity of naturalism, yet, on the very next, contravened or ignored. The vulgar insistence of this contradiction does not yield to semantic refinements: Mr. Edel has still eventually to maintain that

Verena Tarrant and Adam Verver never seem unreal to us, and Mr. Blackmur that neither Kate Croy nor Dr. Sloper ever strikes us as alive; and I do not see how either statement can be taken for true.

The real world of the novelist is of course not the real world the epistemologist fusses over, but a construction within a context. One has to say this in so many words, if only to avoid the affliction of nonsense. Not long ago a Mr. Geismar was sneering at James's Paris in *The Ambassadors* for bearing so little resemblance to the actual Paris of the time, as drawn with such virtuosity by Roger Shattuck in *The Banquet Years*. Yet how on earth could the point ever be that an ageing and inattentive James was so out of touch with reality as to equip his characters with an ambience a quarter-century obsolete? The point is not even whether he knew it. What a character has to fit is not some scene dredged up by sociological fatuity but a writer's schema, his context. To niggle about realism in *this* sense is like asking why, say, Miss Compton-Burnett, once she took it into her head to set her novels in 1880 or thereabouts, didn't write them in the 1880's manner. Such things should be commonplaces. Miss Compton-Burnett settled on the 1880's because she decided, or found, that that scene— its surfaces, its dull-gnomic jargon, the particular convulsions of its decorum, its ethical lucidity—best showed off humanity as she was concerned to show it; she writes there in comfort. But back to the "dilemma."

I propose to argue that its cause is a simple disregard of James's defects as a writer. This might have been the consensus long ago if the academic eye had been trained to see defects as defects. But a professor of literature is not so much trained to *look* at what he is reading as to find things to say about it. Nor by and large does he know *how* writers write. Show him even a piece of James's own self-criticism, something as explicit as

> This whole corner of the picture bristles with "dodges" —such as [a literary critic] should feel himself all committed to recognize and denounce—for disguising the reduced scale of the exhibition, for foreshortening at any cost, for imparting to patches the value of presences, for dressing objects in an *air* as of the dimensions they can't possibly have.
> (Preface to *The Wings of the Dove*)

—show a professor of English literature this, and far from making him "recognize and denounce" the defect, or look for others that James glozed over, it may simply demonstrate to him that his great novelist is a great critic too. James cannot have defects, as writers have, because he was not *just* a writer. Called upon, then, to explain to myself a passage in James that is deficient in naturalism, yet forbidden by habit or incapacity from remarking the nature of its defects, I am bound to say that it is non-naturalistic by Intention; and so in due course propound and erect into a system some portentous doctoral variant of Sir Herbert's "point where moral judgments are formed." Once such a semantic structure is jointed together and in place, one is safe inside it from intrusive considerations of whether James is uneven, or his taste uncertain, or his self-discipline permissive, or his characters either real or unreal, or

even whether his novels are *about* as much as he has
made us believe. One does not see the confused and
paradoxical man, but simply that luminous whole, the
great master. Minor eccentricities, yes. But there can
be no vulgar assessments, as for other writers, of what
the writer was doing: James was doing Something Else.

All this seems to me wrong. I am as tired of the word
"moral" applied to James as of the "compelling" and
"compassionate" that hack reviewers apply to novels—
moral intelligence, moral seriousness, moral intensity,
moral imagination, morally dismissive; I begin to doubt
whether I know what language means. They are trying
to say what makes a great novel great and are not suc-
ceeding: they have simply replaced one adjective with
another and called the result aesthetic description. A
habit of dialectic may comfort the unforbidden soul,
but what is wanted in the case of James is a habit of
making specific judgments about the writing first—and
if need be, line for line. If you are asked to say which of
Housman's famous variants is right,

$$molliaque \begin{Bmatrix} inmittens \\ inmites \end{Bmatrix} fixit\ in\ ora\ manus,[10]$$

dialectics will not help you. Mr. Dupee and Mr. Wilson
have mentioned James's shortcomings here and there,
and so in England has Mr. Leavis, but not in what might
be called journeyman detail. Why does Mr. Wilson tell
us that the first hundred pages of *The Bostonians* are
"in their way, one of the most masterly things that
Henry James ever did," [11] but not what is non-masterly

about the rest of it? Or what, aside from his term "social history," is so masterly about even the first hundred pages? What I want to try here, then, is whether a more straightforward view of James may not emerge if one looks at a couple of his novels not for signs of philosophical intervention but simply to see what they amount to as writing. This is perhaps not so easy as picking *inmites*. But is it much harder—for an educated sensibility—than saying why *inmites* is what one picks?

The grip of biography is so strong upon critics still that I had better say, in advance, that I do not propose to assess James's writing in terms of the psychosymptomatology of why he wrote it—considerations of whether he was oedipally impotent, or had a slipped disc or an undescended testicle, or was discommoded by infibulation, or even was an adroit old queen.[12] Literature may indeed be the encoded arrangement of psychosomatic disorders that fashion insists it is, but its interest does not really lie in the decipherment. Nor, on another level of biography, does it make the slightest difference whether Strether is a portrait of Howells or Miss Theale of Miss Temple. Every word a writer sets down has an antecedent of some sort; how not? But how does discovering it inform us of the quality of what he has written?

2

The Bostonians can serve as my first case-study, and the preface to the Modern Library edition, done for us by Mr. Howe, as a specimen of academic commentary.

Prefaces are of course to some extent advertisement. But this preface is also a perfectly respectable sub-mandarin job that analyzes characterization, explores and explains the action, ticks off relevant symbolism, purveys insights, and by manipulating fashionable noetic tropes of one sort or another (sociology, semantics, and of course Freud) softens the reader up and instructs him in how deeply impressed with this novel he is about to be; in short he is in for a masterpiece. As is current custom, aesthetic or technical assessment gets much less space than professorial ideation; it is not really suggested that aesthetics or technique might be clues to whether a novel was a masterpiece anyhow; so the main rubrics are run through rapidly and, so to speak, for the record—we are given specimens of style, the characterization of the lesbian Miss Chancellor is profound, the tempo slackens somewhat after the first hundred and fifty pages but is this a flaw or just because the scene has shifted from Boston to New York? and so on. Mr. Howe finds very little wrong with the book, but then readers might not believe him if he did ("If it's no good how come they republish it?"). Well, the collected edition did not; but it is never mandarin practice to exhibit qualms about James, and Mr. Howe is not alone in assessing *The Bostonians* high. Mr. Leavis has even set down the grotesque opinion that it and *The Portrait of a Lady* "seem to me the two most brilliant novels in the language." [13] Mr. Howe has, then, given the reader exactly the sort of preface that our college literature-departments have taught us to believe is a full critical summing up. You want to know what the stuff says; what else is there?

The story line of *The Bostonians* is the eventually successful attempt of a seedy young Southern lawyer, Basil Ransom, to take an insipid but beautiful girl-lecturer, Verena Tarrant, away from the rich young Boston spinster she has been living with, Olive Chancellor; as a thematic echo of this action, the young women crusade interminably for the emancipation of woman, which Ransom just as interminably treats as a joke. There is nothing actually unsettling about this somewhat specialized scenario, though James's picking it for his "attempt to show that I *can* write an American story" [14] daunts me. But if it is to come off, then obviously a crucial thing, to be handled with insight and perspicuity, is what goes on between the two girls. This need not be explicit in the manner of the three young women in Miss Stein's *Things As They Are:* a writer can make it as nuancé as suits him. But he must have us see that he knows what he is doing, or not convince.

This, on two planes, James largely fails to do. The less important, the girls' relationship as blue-stockings, remains an unhappy blank. The insistently mentioned readings aloud, the research, the discussions, the plans, the whole "wonderful insight they had obtained into the history of feminine anguish" (Chapter 20), simply have no intellectual content at all. In a writer who was William James's brother, the ignorance of how ideas are handled by people used to handling them is staggering. Nor can this be defended as satire: Miss Tarrant's lectures are not parody but a vacuum. But far more damaging, the girls' emotional relationship is feebly conveyed. The scenes between them, when not merely superficial or ambiguous, are limited to a single aspect of the ménage, Miss Chancellor's jealousy. Emphasis on this is of course necessary as a narrative mechanism: the plot's "conflict" is after all over the possession of Miss Tarrant. But even when the complete emotional content is narrowed down to jealousy, James never properly carries the scenes through. In Chapter 30 a scene even breaks off for lunch. One almost concludes that James stopped because he wasn't clear how to continue the scene as it was developing; and sure enough, when the inquisition of Miss Chancellor's anxiety resumes, the *scène à faire* vaporizes off in a fine spray of woman's-magazine dialogue. Similarly, both the beautifully prepared bitter scene in Chapter 34 (Miss Tarrant has spent the day with Ransom in Central Park) and the ultimate explosion in Chapter 36 (he has asked her to marry him) are shortened far beyond what is defendable—brought rapidly up to a wild burst of tears in each case and then abruptly dropped, abandoned. As to any final stage, what happens to the emotions of two young women when one is seduced away, there is not a sentence to suggest that this is even part of such a story: the whole improbable affair is broken off short, exactly as has been every scene dealing with the course of its passions.

I have mentioned ambiguity. This is not Mr. Wilson's term, but passages like

> She knew that Olive's injunction ["Promise me not to marry!"] ought not to have surprised her; she had already felt it in the air. . . . But . . . the effect of that quick, violent colloquy was to make her nervous and impatient, as if she had had a sudden glimpse of fu-

turity. That was rather awful, even if it represented the fate one would like.

(Chap. 16)

"Ought not to have surprised her"! If Miss Tarrant was surprised then how did she know she ought not to have been? And if she ought not to have been surprised, then what is the rest of the nonsense about? Which, in short, is the reader to decide is the simpleton, Miss Tarrant or James?

The Notebooks show that James himself laid the popular failure of *The Bostonians* to his having tried something that, once in it, he found he couldn't quite do: he was haunted throughout the writing, he told his brother, by "the sense of knowing terribly little about the kind of life I had attempted to describe. . . . I should have been much more rapid and had a lighter hand, with a subject concerned with people and things of a nature more near to my experience." [15] He had had a struggle "to make the picture substantial," he said; and certainly this looks like a good working explanation of why New York, which he knew better, is better portrayed in terms of people and things than Boston. Where in James are the serene non-cerebral natural good manners of Beacon or Mt. Vernon Streets? Where, for that matter, is there a Porcellian?

And yet defective knowledge does not account for anything like all the shortcomings of *The Bostonians;* and in fact James propounded the exculpation so soon after the book appeared that, the egotism of the creative artist being what it is, self-defense is a likelier motive than self-criticism. As a minor example, it is not defects

of knowledge that make the "comic" characters ludicrous or absurd rather than comic: they are not amusing
but just socially ungainly; the bumpkin joke was em-
phatically not for James, yet there it is, page after depressing page, confidently presented to us as satire. A
far worse, indeed fatal, blemish is the book's preposterous climax, a two-chapter scene unmatched in James for
dramatic silliness, unlikelihood, and plain vulgarity.
Ransom is made to burst into the back-stage of a great
auditorium packed with Bostonian élite, come to be
improved by Miss Tarrant's eloquence; he windily re-
capitulates every argument he has already spent the
book inflicting on his young woman and on us, while
beyond the proscenium the brilliant audience impa-
tiently whistles and stamps; and at long last snatches her
from her out-ranted and swooning backers and rushes
her forth into the triumphant night. This is trash and
nothing but trash, and defective knowledge had singularly little to do with it.

Nor at the very center of the story, the girls' ménage,
does defective knowledge strike me as correctly defining
what in James's handling went wrong. What is not "substantial" is not so much the girls' misunderstood relationship as the picture of each girl as a girl. Miss Chancellor fails by being static. She puts one a little in mind
of those Dickens characters with far-fetched but pictur-
esque tics, tics used to prompt the memory as to which
character is which as they reappear. Miss Chancellor's
tic is functional but it is still a tic, a kind of syndrome
of neurotic detail which regularly accompanies her en-
trances—abruptness, social distress, and the like. Yet

when James lets us see what is going on inside her head (the famous point of view, in *The Bostonians,* skips unconcernedly about from character to character) there is singularly little evidence of neurosis. Indeed most of the interplay of Miss Chancellor's psyche with Miss Tarrant's has the chattering analytical vacuity of a woman's page. What James must have done is report the behavior of some specific young woman he had seen and carefully observed; and, I should suggest, diagnosed also; but as he had seen her only in social situations, her social conduct was all he could describe. "The power to guess the unseen from the seen" that he praises in *The Art of Fiction,* the ability "to judge the whole piece by the pattern," is not the same thing as creating it.

James's failure with the Tarrant character is of a different sort altogether. Horace once admonished the Piso brothers not to draw mermaids if what they had in mind was a picture of a girl or a fish; but by 1885 James may have forgotten the precept along with the Latin. Miss Tarrant, if one may without offense describe a Boston girl with an ablative absolute, is *undique collatis membris.* One part of her is the basic Jamesian girl, though with less mind of her own than his standard; the other part is "the little prophetess," the lower-middle-class girl-lecturer-cum-medium, with all the shabby paraphernalia of the lyceum circuit about her. No writer who ever lived could combine those two aspects into a character he could work with. It is as if Mark Twain had made Huck a boy inventor.[16] James's difficulty was a programmatic one that a writer of twenty years' experience ought to have avoided automatically: Miss Tarrant was planned in advance, for serialization, but so badly planned that he only discovered something was wrong when he was too far along to change her. Moreover he failed to see *what* was wrong, and consequently tried to remedy whatever it was by tossing in any random "substantial" traits that might give an impression of reality. He thus added to the unfusable double-character of his heroine pieces of behavior that hardly belonged to either side of it, and that are even contradictory. Thus she becomes by turns a simpleton, or a hypocrite, or suspiciously close to mercenary, or still again of the "incurable softness" that led Mr. Dupee to misclassify her as "nearly blank." [17] It was this kind of creative desperation that produced such indecisive nonsense as

> she answered, with her sweet, vain laugh, but apparently with perfectly good faith.
>
> (Chap. 18)

or, with embarrassed parentheses added to the same telltale pair of words,

> (there was no one like Verena for making speeches apparently flirtatious, with the best faith and the most innocent intention in the world) . . .
>
> (Chap. 33)

"Verena was of many pieces" (Chapter 18) is in fact an unwitting paraphrase of the *variae plumae* Horace so justly warned the Pisones against; and by Chapter 37 James's own psyche had so far lost patience with him as to make him blurt out that the girls' ménage was "so singular on Verena's part in particular that I despair of presenting it to the reader with the air of reality."

47

In a word, the central drama of *The Bostonians* depends on two unrealized characters, joined under emotional conditions that are not conveyed, in an intellectual endeavor whose intellectual content is zero.

It is not then surprising to find parallel deficiencies in the writing itself. The best one can say about the style of *The Bostonians* is that it may be transitional; the worst, and the more accurate, is that on the whole it is dreadful. The rapid polyhedral hard clarity and functional epigram of James's writing in *Washington Square* —"limpid intensity" is Mr. Dupee's admirable description of it [18]—has here lost both its lucidity and its speed, and any kind of elegance, while the impressionist diction and the entrechats of logaoedic rhythm that James eventually worked his way to are still years ahead. As a result, page after page confronts one with sentences of an ineptness past all belief from a writer of parts with two decades of professional experience already behind him. They are not only bad, but bad with variety, and sometimes they are silly as well. I doubt if there is a more fatuous sentence in American literature than

> "Murder, what a lovely voice!" he exclaimed, involuntarily.
>
> (Chap. 35)

One need no longer wonder where the author of *Tom Swift* learned his graces of style.* Or again,

* Though all Homers nod. The sentence *"By Jove! this won't do," cried Tom, throwing himself into a chair with a hearty laugh* can be assigned at sight to *The Rover Boys.* Or for *Tom* read *Alyosha* and it is Mrs. Garnett translating Dostoyevski. Yet in fact it was written, in Chapter 13 of *Mansfield Park,* by the elegant Miss Austen.

By this time a certain agitation was perceptible; several ladies, impatient of vain delay, had left their places, to appeal personally to Mrs. Farrinder, who was presently surrounded by sympathetic remonstrants.

(Chap. 6)

Or still again,

These meditations accompanied him in his multifarious wanderings through the streets and suburbs of the New England capital.

(Chap. 13)

The lapse of time has changed connotations; in 1885 a hero could be assigned a name like Merton Densher because there was no word for false teeth but false teeth, and when Miss Challoner asks Miss Tarrant, "Did Mr. Burrage try to make love to you?" we adjust our minds and do not understand her to suggest that he flung Miss Tarrant down on a studio couch and tried to tear her clothes off. But fancy anybody, genius or not, in the 1880's or in any decade, trying to deal with the intricate misgivings of the human heart through a miasma of sentences like

She loved, she was in love—she felt it in every throb of her being.

(Chap. 38)

or like

"Good God! that I should make her suffer like this!" said Ransom to himself.

(Chap. 42)

Equally bad are the mere technical lapses. There is sheer structural clumsiness, spoiling the wit, in

> This phenomenon occurred when the vapours of social ambition mounted to her brain, when she extended an arm from which a crumpled dressing-gown fluttered back to seize the passing occasion.
>
> (Chap. 6)

or (not spoiling much of anything)

> He knew what he intended about her sharing the noon-day repast with him somehow.
>
> (Chap. 33)

The otiose sentence is everywhere. Miss Tarrant cannot be fetched a glass of water without our being told why water is what was fetched; and a chapter that contains one of the best scenes in the book opens with the insufferable irrelevance:

> The hour that Olive proposed to Mrs. Burrage, in a note sent early the next morning, for the interview to which she consented to lend herself, was the stroke of noon; this period of the day being chosen in consequence of a prevision of many subsequent calls upon her time. She remarked in her note that she did not wish any carriage to be sent for her, and she surged and swayed up the Fifth Avenue on one of the convulsive, clattering omnibuses which circulate in that thoroughfare.
>
> (Chap. 32)

There is, finally, the vice James was never free from, the over-use of metaphor for what he must have thought of as the invigoration of the passage before him. Where Homer expanded James distorts and distends, and never oftener than when the paragraph is flaccid or flat: it calls for *something,* God knows, and what it gets is a *stucco duro* of surface decoration.

> Olive had taken her up, in the literal sense of the phrase, like a bird of the air, had spread an extraordinary pair of wings, and carried her through the dizzying void of space. Verena liked it, for the most part; liked to shoot upward without an effort of her own and look down upon all creation, upon all history, from such a height.
>
> (Chap. 11)

The heavy sentences take on a megatherian life of their own: whatever else was going on stops, for James as for his reader, until the thing has rumbled past.

How is one to explain all this dismal stuff? I have suggested stylistic flux; he was forty-two but late in maturing, and beyond doubt his early style now seemed bare for what was becoming his taste; moreover finding a style to handle his growing complexities, in a day when literary jargon and indeed language was as rigid as in 1885, was for a man as conventional as James a very long process of painful trial and apologetic error. But in *The Bostonians* my guess is that he was also unnerved by his inability to diagnose what was going wrong with the book as he worked at it. When this happens a writer can go to pieces on every page, and his taste becomes wholly unreliable. If this happened to James at a moment of stylistic indecision anyhow, the rubbish I have quoted would be a natural result.

Yet through the general and pervasive fog an occasional sentence nevertheless shows James groping toward the impressionism he later handled with such skill and affection:

> Strange I call the nature of her reflections, for they softly battled with each other as she listened, in the warm, still air, touched with the far-away hum of the immense city, to his deep, sweet, distinct voice, expressing monstrous opinions with exotic cadences and mild, familiar laughs, which, as he leaned towards her, almost tickled her cheek and ear.
>
> (Chap. 33)

Ten years later James would have re-worked the latter part of this sentence into congruence with the opening phrases; but even as it stands one can see him glimpsing what words can do, to convey, to render, to move, rather than merely state.

So much for a bad novel. Now what about a good one?

3

The novels of James's last period have to be examined in a different way. There is far more to admire, and a great deal that is absolutely masterly; and in consequence one has to look at a work chapter by chapter rather than, as with *The Bostonians*, merely by aspects. Otherwise the combination of mature brilliance and mature glibness—his "dodges"—will carry one's judgment along bemused and beaming: everything will tend to look of a piece, and we shall be back in academia.

This chapter-by-chapter scrutiny is what I shall try with *The Golden Bowl*.

I have taken this rather than *The Wings of the Dove* because its contrasts are so much sharper, and rather than *The Ambassadors* because there, in complete agreement with Mr. Leavis,[19] I cannot find anything to admire at all. Women perhaps find it more readable than men do. One trouble, technically, is that male characters, which are never what James did best, take up so much of the total wordage. In particular, the Jamesian-male shilly-shally of Strether is excessive, and the endless bleating of Bilham is really not to be borne at all. Again, the love affair which James's plan puts at the center of his action is both a sensory and a narrative blank: there is not even enough physical presence bestowed on Mme. de Vionnet to suggest that she had ever been in anybody's bedroom. The choral commentary of Bilham (with hemichoria by Maria Gostrey) is as crude as it is wearisome, mere third-person narration disguised as dialogue: nowhere is Mr. Wilson's cruel phrase "the fumes of Jamesian gas" more just or more apropos. One is even exasperated by opportunities programmatically thrown away—Miss Gostrey starts off beautifully only to fade into a mere annotation upon the action, yet how could anyone overlook the sheer comedy of making her the American parallel of Mme. de Vionnet and seduce Strether? And so on. The ladies can have it.

The Golden Bowl tells how the marriage of an Italian prince and a very rich young American girl, Maggie Verver, is brought into shadow by his renewing a clandestine earlier affair with her friend, the former Charlotte Stant, now married to Miss Verver's father; the story ends with nothing acknowledged yet every heart known. Whether this is a masterpiece is part of what we are engaged in considering, but at all events it is a Jamesian masterpiece. The situation is unlikely but credible, as by and large are the characters and what they do; the riches of incantation, the mature conception, the haze of hallucination of every kind, are beyond anything in *The Bostonians*. The book is above all alive.

Yet of the final trio of novels, *The Golden Bowl* has by far the feeblest opening; one could in fact call its first chapter a kind of prefabricated failure. In *The Wings of the Dove* the very first words are "She waited, Kate Croy," and as that enchanting young creature waits James starts breathing life into her (she fidgets, leafs through a magazine, makes mouths at herself in a glass, etc.), whereupon, from her, the whole opening takes on an instantaneous life. In much the same way the first chapter of *The Ambassadors* comes alive from Maria Gostrey—as would *The Golden Bowl* have done from the immediate presence of Charlotte Stant. These three young women are of a type that James clearly knew, despite our biographical ignorance of how, with a kind of physical intimacy beyond anything else in his work. It is his sensual awareness of them that endows them and every scene they take part in with life. But in the first chapter of *The Golden Bowl* we have, instead, only a young multi-millionairess who is still pure cardboard and what is for the moment the most inert Italian prince in literature (a literature that contains Fabrice del Dongo!), and James has provided these creatures with dialogue empty and frigid enough for the conventional butler and parlormaid dusting their expository way around the set as the curtain rises on one more well-made play.

A writer with less personal ritual about his preliminary schemata would have revised this chapter beyond recognition. One normally reads a draft through every twenty thousand words or so for congruence, for flow; and at that point the shock of disparity, the difference in mere aliveness, between this first chapter and the five that follow would have set any less inflexible novelist to immediate recasting. The particular and vital thing James has failed to convey is the relationship between Miss Verver and her affianced Prince: we should be made to know it as unmistakably as, in Chapter 3, James sets the secret and unforgetting closeness of the Prince and Miss Stant before us out of their past. It was still an era of convention: at balls in 1903 a young man had still to deliver his partner back to her chaperone after each dance, and the written dialogue of the engaged couple was, for a novelist, similarly circumscribed. But it is not Edwardian behavior that is James's trouble here: it is simply that Miss Verver and the Prince cannot be said to have any discernible feelings about each other whatever. She is hardly even present, physically; and if the reader is to see her as the equal of her lovely rival, she should be shown in love, to the full limit of Edwardian candor, and perhaps even glowingly.

If, loving, we enjoye not, wee
Not Bodies, but Idea's, *be;*

and even assuming that the idea was indeed James's lamented cousin Miss Temple, and Miss Verver in consequence more alive to him from the start than to us, it is still astonishing that he did not see the dramatic risks in postponing—for a hundred thousand words!—words haunted moreover by the most enchanting "adventuress" he ever put on paper—our awareness that he had conceived the future wife as countervailing emotionally against the mistress.

Yet then comes one of the finest sequences anywhere in James. In five chapters the old master launches his story with solidness and speed, and with a virtuosity of characterization that makes the opening chapter seem to have been by another hand. In Chapter 2 the Prince's call on Mrs. Assingham blocks in the background for Miss Stant's entrance; and in Chapter 3 she appears—

> If when she moved off she looked like a huntress, she looked when she came nearer like his notion, perhaps not wholly correct, of a muse.

—in a scene of superb intensity that manages to suggest both her past and her future affairs with him through the suave amenities of dialogue in the present. The Prince takes on life too: there is an electric difference between his sensibility and behavior with Miss Stant in Chapters 3, 5, and 6 and with Miss Verver in Chapter 1. The past is filled in in more detail in Chapter 4, in the first of those choral commentaries, the duets of Colonel and Mrs. Assingham. Finally, in Chapters 5 and 6, the Prince and Miss Stant meet alone, telling no one; and as they shop for her wedding-present for Miss Verver, and come on the Bowl, their whole deep and unending intimacy little by little unfolds before our eyes. There are minor details in these five chapters that are eccentric, but within what might be called normal Jamesian limits; and if the bowl as symbol is of the dreariest banality [20] at least it is not, here, obtrusive. The sequence reads, in a word, like a sequence from a masterpiece; and if James owes its success, technically, to the luminous young huntress who is its center, then she was indeed—and he must have known it—his muse.

And my guess is, she was. It is not just that girls like Miss Croy and Miss Stant come more easily to life because the plots make them active (they seduce), while the Miss Ververs are assigned very little to *do* (except pine), and this makes for pallor. It is, much more, that the happy ease and flow and effortless life with which he does his "adventuresses" comes from a creator's delight. He adored them: one has only to listen to the caress of

> He knew her narrow hands, he knew her long fingers and the shape and colour of her finger-nails, he knew the special beauty of movement and line when she turned her back.
>
> (*The Golden Bowl,* Chap. 3)

This is as sensual for James as Cummings's "the slim hinging you" and

> *your body's suddenly
> curving entire warm questions* [21]

in bed with him across from the Ile de la Cité. Somewhere or other a Charlotte Stant must, in Propertius's phrase, have plundered James's senses, as his heroine-archetype Miss Temple seems not to have done. "He knew." I am not concerned with biography, or insisting that the warmth and confidence and the sheer knowledge of his adventuress portraits implies a series of high-style clandestinities which his famous secretiveness has succeeded in covering over. I am talking about how the creative mind works; and I merely say that if you ask, What did James's psyche *like* to write about, the answer is: about pretty and poised young women, and in particular young women who, as we now say, had been around. An analogous delight is what makes Mrs. Burrage in *The Bostonians* so brilliant a picture of the well-bred New York society woman—the voice, the style, the manner impeccably done, the distinction rendered to perfection, as alive as any of her identical great-granddaughters one can meet on the same Upper East Side today. She is in fact the most "substantial" character in the novel, and a scene flowers into life when she enters it.

The Jamesian perfection of Chapters 2 through 6, however, makes all the more depressing the equally Jamesian shortcomings of the three that follow. Here, for more than twelve thousand words, *everything* stops —for a cluttered and interminable character-sketch of that "small, spare, slightly stale person, deprived of the general prerogative of presence," Miss Verver's multimillionaire father. I do not pretend to know what moral exquisitenesses of design the academic mind advances to itself for James's spending so disproportionate a time on the least operative of his four main characters. I suggest however that the disproportion masks an inverse disproportion of assurance: Adam Verver is not just the least operative character but also, for reasons it upset James to face, the least realizable. James's style has a tell-tale habit. When he was sure of what he was doing he sped along, his hand rapid and light: he didn't "bother about the writing," if I may use Sir Herbert's strange phrase in controversion of what Sir Herbert meant by it; Chapters 2 through 6 are typical of that fluidity and confident ease. But when a section was not going well, and he knew it wasn't but not why, there set in the anxious over-elaboration that he described to his brother as occurring in *The Bostonians,* a kind of compositional outflanking or verbal circumnavigation around whatever felt wrong; and if this took three or four times the wordage, well, he was past the obstacle and safe—the only acknowledgement of his dissimulation a passing phrase of apology when the long-windedness has been excessive:

> the occasion round which we have perhaps drawn our circle too wide . . .
>
> (Chap. 8)

meaning no less than seven thousand words on Verver's sneaking off to the billiard-room.

With Mr. Verver, as most Jamesists have seen but few admitted, the difficulty, at least on the surface of things, is that the character doesn't even begin to fit the part. The part is that of a self-made multi-millionaire widower of forty-seven; aggressive, peremptory, predatory, and a brilliant money-maker; internationally known, moreover, as the most epicurean and imperial of art collectors; in a word, one of the opulent of the earth. But *in* this role James cast a character whom he went out of his way to *mis*cast. It is not just that we are asked to believe of a fabulously rich and powerful man that he

> bethought himself of his personal advantage, in general, only when it might appear to him that other advantages, those of other persons, had successfully put in their claim.
>
> (Chap. 7)

To this wild and dismaying unlikelihood James expressly, and insistently, adds *ridicule.* He not only sprinkles diminutives of every kind over Verver's character and appearance as skillfully as Joyce did over Chandler's in *A Little Cloud,* but piles up disparaging detail that Joyce carefully left out. Verver is not just diffident, apprehensive, and socially inconspicuous—he is a pottering dim little pre-elderly nonentity. He has no friends; no acquaintances; even what a Roman would have called his *clientes* are dingy—when he rents a splendid English country house nobody comes to visit but a repellent middle-class American widow named Rance and a pair of spinster sisters with the equally unappetizing name of Lutch. Worse still, James does not stop at marrying him off to a girl who for two solid chapters has given him every warning possible to decent Edwardian dialogue that another man (his own son-in-law!) is making up her mind for her, but climaxes even these scenes of proleptic infidelity by having Verver *rejoice* at it!

> She held her [telegram] wide open, but her eyes were all for his. "It isn't Maggie. It's the Prince."
> "I *say!*"—he gaily rang out. "Then it's the best of all."
> (Chap. 13)

What under heaven is the point of all this belittlement? Granted that no man in his senses would enter into the marriage James's plot has set up, and that Verver's behavior is a picture less of life as our Creator thought it up than of that special predestination, the Jamesian schema—still even on that plane two questions stand unresolved. (1) Why not plan in the first place a character to *fit* the schema? A conventionally Morgan-partnerlike financial pirate was perfectly workable: it would have been no trick to present him as *radouci*, even *ramolli* for that matter, into a tender, indulgent, sensitive father, if that was in fact James's controlling consideration. (2) Why in any event make the character —of all possible qualities!—*ridiculous?* For this completely contravenes the schema: it is all very well to prepare the reader in a well-made way for the lamentable adultery to come, but what happens to its dramatic function, to its very status, if the preparation keeps reminding one of some stale French joke? (There is perhaps only one cuckoldry in modern literature that is more botched and unbelievable, Ford Madox Ford's *The Good Soldier,* where the situation is too preposterous even to describe.) The fact seems to be that even critics of the first rank pretty much give up on Mr. Verver: one finds Mr. Blackmur reduced to phrases like

> At least this interpretation of Verver's acts seems implicit in what James allows us to see of this little . . . old man.[22]

Where Mr. Blackmur groped for explanation, the rest of us can assume there is not very much to find. In *this* portrait, James has merely been *tenax praeposteri*.

And so one might go through the remaining two-thirds of *The Golden Bowl*. Chapters 17 and 18, for example, leading up to that remarkable kiss of recommitment of the new Mrs. Verver and the Prince, are, despite flaws, well over on the plus side; Chapter 22, when their old affair actually begins again, certainly in part deserves Mr. Crews's ridicule.[23] Sometimes the Assingham chorus is handled deftly, even with drama; sometimes, as in the middle of Chapter 24, it sinks back to Bilham-level. There is the whole thrashed-over ambiguity of Verver's relationship to his daughter and what *did* James mean. And so on. The masterly and the manqué alternate, among the merely ordinary and expected ups and downs of craftsmanship.

What part in all this, then, does style play?

James's first project for *The Golden Bowl,* in his notebook on 14 February 1895, contains the sentence, "I seem to see it as a nominal 60,000 words: which *may* become 75,000." This is a practical and a sensible estimate. But when in 1902–03 he came to the actual writing, there took place what one might call (more politely than Mr. Wilson) the Jamesian intervention, and his eventual wordage rose toward the quarter-million. A writer says what he has to say as tersely as it can be said well; and this, in his early novels, James followed his Continental models in paying attention to. But by the time he was sixty, the line between the expressive and the garrulous was not one he took pleasure in drawing: on the contrary, his habit had become the sort of thing he describes in his project for *The Ivory Tower:*

> I seem to see already how my action, however tightly packed down, will strain my Ten Books, most blessedly, to cracking.

Never mind sardonic comment on that "most blessedly"; it is the self-deception of the "tightly packed down" that is the symptom. He must simply no longer have seen loquacity for what it was: *every* word he set down was essential to expounding the action, *every* movement of his sensibility had become "the most magnificent masterly little vivid economy." There is, I suggest, a clear connection between his reputation as a talker and his later style: much of this is less writing than simply chat, with the rhythms, the sentence-structure, the psychic anacoloutha, the vocabulary, approaching those of conversation. In parts of *The Ambassadors* and *The Golden Bowl* this looseness is even proposed to us as a technical discovery, as in the Bilham and Assingham choruses. One of the seductions (and snares) of these escapes into the spurious first person is that when a writer comes on something difficult he need not face and solve the difficulty, but can run around and all over it as one does in conversation, and save by writing half a dozen sentences the trouble of composing one. *Si je me laisse entraîner le moins du monde,* Constant lamented in his journal, *et qu'il y survienne le moindre obstacle, je me connais, ma tête part, et Dieu sait tout ce qu'il en résulterait.*[24] Constant was talking about pretty women; but an empty sheet of paper can be a very pretty thing too. The phrase James used (of something else) in Chapter 18 of *The Golden Bowl* extenuates, but it does not absolve:

> The whole demonstration . . . presented itself as taking place at a very high level of debate—in the cool upper air of the finer discrimination, the deeper sincerity, the larger philosophy.

The phrase itself partakes of the very glibness it could be quoted to excuse.

It is perhaps this self-indulgence that makes James's style seem at times to be, as is often argued or implied,[25] an end in itself. For it must appear that little but an obsession with rhetoric can explain passages like

> [the day] was one of those for which you had to be, blessedly, an American—as indeed you had to be, blessedly, an American for all sorts of things: so long as you hadn't, blessedly or not, to remain in America.
> (*The Golden Bowl*, Chap. 5)

This, in its context, has no function; it could hardly have a function in any context; even therefore if one can't imagine its style's giving pleasure to anybody but

James himself, what, if not style, can its point be? Yet his notebooks quite clearly show his mind to have been predominantly on other things—the action, the plot, the manner, the method, the semantic implication; and when in his preface to *The Wings of the Dove* he says that "my use of windows and balconies is doubtless at best an extravagance by itself," he is not talking about style but of massing detail for mood and indirect presentation.

Self-indulgence in writers is of two quite distinct kinds. In the first place, the born writer is almost always a gross sensualist, and quite simply *likes* irrelevant decoration as such; it makes up for having to write the bread-and-butter passages that in narrative cannot sometimes be avoided. One kind is James's lovely impressionist sentence

> Venice glowed and plashed and called and chimed again; the air was like a clap of hands, and the scattered pinks, yellows, blues, sea-greens, were like a hanging out of vivid stuffs, a laying down of fine carpets.
>
> (*The Wings of the Dove*, Chap. 32)

Another kind is Henry Green's recurrent doves, or his ballrooms of waltzing girls in *Loving* and *Concluding*, or even his giving them all names that begin with M. Still another kind is Miss Compton-Burnett's indulging herself by having in every novel, quite as unnecessarily and unfunctionally, at least two characters whose speech is a fusillade of epigrams. These kinds of decoration are among the glories of writing, and a kind of self-indulgence a writer ought to be indulged in.

But the kind behind things like the blessedly-American passage has a very different inspiration. It is what occurs when a writer has not quite brought himself to look at what he knows lies just ahead, and is filling in time till forced to. He may not have decided quite how it is to go, or will go best. Or—more probably—the Whatever-it-is that feeds phrasing and all else through to his conscious mind from wherever-it-is, is idling, or is bored, or wants to do something else, or is planning the seduction of some girl, and anyhow still isn't ready to let him have what comes next (which it may have had ready for weeks). To dissemble this inactivity, it feeds him something else; anything else; relevant or not, and usually not; simply something he can proceed at meantime with what will look like a clear conscience. A man as used to manipulating language as James was can shape a blessedly-American sentence as automatically—as mindlessly and as meaninglessly—as a pastry-chef squeezes rosettes from a pastry-bag. And in *this* form of "inspiration" the writer's self-indulgence consists in letting the rubbish he has written stand.

James's later style is a rather more complex subject than any Jamesist seems to see. The Venice sentence is, of course, one kind of thing that is admirable in it; descriptions of scene and atmosphere are something James nearly always did well, and here it has the perfection of maturity. Another kind is a sentence singled out by Mr. Auchincloss,[26] with a craftsman's sensitivity, in A. C. Benson's anecdote of a chance meeting with James just before James died:

He put his hand on my arm and said: "My dear Arthur, my mind is so constantly and continuously bent upon you in wonder and good will that any change in my attitude could be only the withholding of a perpetual and settled felicitation." He uttered his little determined, triumphant laugh, [Benson concludes] and I saw him no more.

Now this may well be Benson's memory polishing what James actually said; any experienced journalist would be sure it was, and probably be right. I offer it merely as style. This exquisite (and moving) sentence is James conveying the intricacy of human relationships at the urbane top of his bent, the arabesques of sound and rhythm an angelic counterpart of the sensibility behind what is being both said and implied. A third kind of mastery is his dialogue, which at its best is that polished and heightened sort one finds in the best English short stories, where every speech has a sharp, specific purpose, because it has been *worked* at. Mrs. Verver in Chapter 18 says to the Prince,

"What will you say . . . that you've been doing?"

and we have not only the whole illicit furtiveness of love, but the two of them stand before us in the practiced and unrepented intimacy of their past, so soon and so much more illicitly to be renewed. This is the very opposite of the Jamesian loquacity. It is moreover a compression that James could use in narrative too:

They concealed their pursuit of the irrelevant by the charm of their manner; they took precautions for a courtesy that they had formerly left to come of itself; often, when he had quitted her, he stopped short, walking off, with the aftersense of their change.

(*The Wings of the Dove*, Chap. 38)

The sheer balanced perfection the ear finds in the movement of this sentence can even be borne out statistically.[27]

Yet formidable as the accomplishments of his style are its vices—the addiction to cliché, the laziness, the self-indulgences, the uncertainties of taste, the sheer carelessness and lack of discipline. Here is a typical sentence picked at random in Chapter 20 of *The Golden Bowl:*

> What with the noble fairness of the place, meanwhile, the generous mood of the sunny, gusty, lusty English April, all panting and heaving with impatience, or kicking and crying, even, at moments like some infant Hercules who wouldn't be dressed; what with these things and the bravery of youth and beauty, the insolence of fortune and appetite so diffused among his fellow-guests that the poor Assinghams, in their comparatively marked maturity and their comparatively small splendour, were the only approach to a false note in the concert, the stir of the air was such, for going, in a degree, to one's head, that, as a matter of exposure, almost grotesque in its flagrancy, his situation resembled some elaborate practical joke carried out at his expense.

It is hard to know whether to call this a muddle or a midden, but unmistakably, in detail, it is odds and ends. It begins with an iambic pentameter; and if this is unconscious as well as bad luck in prose, the line is a good line all the same, even majestic and sonorous; it might almost have come out of *The Tempest.* But then James tries out (and regrettably leaves *in*) four adjectives describing April in England, none of them particularly interesting or even descriptive. So to rescue the thing he flings in what must be the ten-thousandth specimen of the Jamesian false-hearty ("all *x*-ing and *y*-ing"); and *this* lures him into ending the colon with a grotesque piece of whimsy. In forty words we have come from the noble fairness of the place to diapers on the infant Hercules. The reader has moreover somewhat lost his place in all this, so the construction is started all over again, oddly enough with another Elizabethan echo (one almost reads "the insolence of fortune and men's eyes"). But James doesn't notice that the reader needs another kind of reminder as well and writes "his" instead of "the Prince's." This colon ends in two kinds of cliché: no one can "approach" a false note but a piano-tuner. But that the colon *has* ended, and that "the stir" starts the main clause, is so instantly obscured by the twitter of

> was such, for going, in a degree, to one's head, that, as a matter of . . .

that not one reader in ten will by this time have the unbewildered concentration to understand what the end of the sentence is even about. I am not sure I am that tenth reader myself. Here in a word are half a dozen styles in fifteen lines, hardly one of them suited to James's purpose or to the moment.

The other novels of the final trio are of a piece; I will take, again, a random sentence from each.

> People were by this time quite scattered, and many of those who had so liberally manifested in calls, in cards, in evident sincerity about visits, later on, over the land, had positively passed in music out of sight.
>
> *(The Wings of the Dove,* Chap. 14)

Here are a couple of typical faults—the little preciosity of using "manifested" intransitively is a tiresome false scent (one expects to find a direct object after "visits" and so ends up having to read the sentence all over again), and the perfectly meaningless "positively" ought for the thousandth time to have been more than even its author's own nerves could stand. I myself am willing to put up with the three alliterations and with "passed in music," but this is no doubt my indulgence.

> Strether read, on the instant, his story—how, astir for the previous hour, the sprinkled newness of the day, so pleasant, at that season, in Paris, he was fairly panting with the pulse of adventure and had been with Mrs. Pocock, unmistakably, to the Marché aux Fleurs.
>
> *(The Ambassadors,* Chap. 26)

"The sprinkled newness of the day" is James at his best: the whole fresh morning is caught in it. But "fairly panting with the pulse of adventure" is inflated and plummy, and is a mixed metaphor; and the word "adventure"—of a stroll with a woman described as James has been describing Mrs. Pocock—is so grisly a choice that the mind reels.

But most damaging of all are the repellent rhythms that this professional cultivator of rhythms has let stand. How is it *possible* not to see—

> *Strether read, on the instant, his story—*
> *How, astir for the previous hour,*
> *He had gone for a walk; and what's more, he*
> *Acquired in the process a flower*

—"a buttonhole freshly adorned with a magnificent rose," James records. We then leave Longfellow for

> *The sprinkled newness of the day,*
> *So pleasant, at this season,*
> *Made James prosodically gay*
> *Without prosodic reason.*

The carelessness is past belief. Even at a climax like the point in Chapter 19 of *The Golden Bowl* at which Mrs. Verver and the Prince start at long last to renew their affair, James could not merely write but *let stand*

> They were silent at first, only facing and faced, only grasping and grasped, only meeting and met.

Much of James's bad writing may have come from his mistaking what he called "the flatness of mere statement" [28] for the flatness of flat statement. This seems the likeliest explanation for such dizzying misuses of metaphor as

> So, therefore, while the minute lasted, it passed between them that their cup was full; which cup their

very eyes, holding it fast, carried and steadied and began, as they tasted it, to praise.

(The Golden Bowl, Chap. 20)

(Even the unconscious prosody is confused—an *Idylls of
the King* pentameter seems to be preceded by a rem-
iniscence of *Verweile doch, du bist so schön.*) False
metaphor is also no doubt back of things like the un-
verb in

> Some such words as those were what *didn't* ring out . . .
>
> (The Golden Bowl, Chap. 25)

Sometimes it leads him into writing phrases that are
clearly in someone else's style altogether, like

> the shining shops that sharpened the grin of solicitation
> on the mask of night.
>
> (The Golden Bowl, Chap. 12)

Metaphor seems to have resulted from a habit, when he
felt a passage turning dull under his pen, not of rewriting what was dull but of adding embellishment to the
dullness. In Chapter 23 of *The Golden Bowl* a sentence
happened to end with the words "a consciousness of
deep waters." Even James saw this as a cliché. But rather
than admit it, and re-write, why not disguise it? and sure
enough, it is transformed into an intentional cue for a
monstrous Homeric simile:

> She [Mrs. Assingham] had been out on these waters, for
> him, visibly; and his tribute to the fact had been his
> keeping her, even if without a word, well in sight. He
> had not quitted for an hour, during her adventure, the

shore of the mystic lake; he had on the contrary stationed himself where she could signal him at need. Her need would have arisen if the planks of her bark had parted—*then* some sort of plunge would have become his immediate duty. His present position, clearly, was that of seeing her in the centre of her sheet of dark water, and of wondering if her actual mute gaze at him didn't perhaps mean that her planks *were* now parting. He held himself so ready that it was quite as if the inward man had pulled off coat and waistcoat. Before he had plunged, however—that is before he had uttered a question—he perceived, not without relief, that she was making for land. He watched her steadily paddle, always a little nearer, and at last he felt her boat bump.

All that these mountains of rubbish signify is that Mrs. Assingham is wondering to herself whether the Prince and Mrs. Verver are sleeping together again. I find the explanatory gloss "that is, before he had uttered a question" especially ludicrous. All this in his final masterpiece!

A man with any eye for style must, it seems to me, find himself continually baffled that anybody who could on occasion write as well as James, could also have left so much sheer barbarism unrevised.

> The announcement made her from home had, in the act, cost some biting of his pen to sundry parts of him.
>
> (*The Golden Bowl,* Chap. 13)

Or, again,

> he could perfectly put his finger on the moment it had taken the bit in its teeth.
>
> (*The Ambassadors,* Chap. 16)

The "it" here happens not to be the finger, but what have grammatical antecedents to do with it? There are times when James's whole relationship to the way he is setting something down cannot even be guessed at. Is he even listening to what he's saying? And why on earth are the passages that have no flaws so few? Why are the extremes of bad and good *so* extreme, the misses so *wide* of the mark? This is the "dilemma."

4

James looked at by a professor of literature is one thing; by a writer, another; by a critic who is both, still a third; and of the vagaries of each there is no end either. Sir Herbert tells me that "it needs a temper of metaphysical disillusion" to appreciate the nighttown episode of *Ulysses;* [29] I am left agape at my innocence of the pre- requisite. Mr. Blackmur discriminates the adultery of *The Ambassadors* ("lovely aspiring") from the adultery of *The Golden Bowl* ("hideous intolerable"),[30] and I am as lost intellectually as if he had not been one of the first critics alive but merely one of his colleagues: adul- tery for the novelist is characters who commit it, not something ominous and halachistic out of the Deca- logue. Mr. Leavis writes [31]

> It is a measure of our sense of the greatness of Henry James's genius that discussion should tend to stress mainly what he failed to do with it.

—when in fact it is a measure of our critical inattention that the sheer aesthetic confusion behind such a sentence should have remained not merely unanalyzed but even unnoticed. *What* is the failure? *How* great is the greatness?

The critical consensus about James is a structure that varies somewhat with the individual critic, but it always tends to rest eventually on two concepts, "master craftsman" and "profound." This being so, the concept "failure" is excluded by definition; and *this* being so, a specific shortcoming, if noticed, cannot be seen for what it is, but must be referred back and described in terms of mastery or profundity, or an august mixture of both. There is accordingly no practical reason for looking at a thing like style: *ex proposito* one expects not bad writing but great meaning. Whenever critics are made uneasy by what James is doing as a writer they can take it that he is thinking; and even the late Mr. Matthiessen, one of the few critics who did take the trouble to look at some of James's re-writing for the New York edition, could blandly talk about "the finally assured confidence of the master craftsman that he is going to realize his potentialities to the full," [32] without apparent reflection that our chief source for the information that James was a master craftsman was James himself, and that the confidence here was unjustified. Nor is the inflation merely one of making him, by gratuitous increments of cerebration, a greater craftsman than he was: the cerebration is inflated too, and Mr. Leavis is completely right in saying

We have, characteristically, in reading him, a sense that important choices are in question and that our finest discrimination is being challenged, while at the same time we can't easily produce for discussion any issues that have moral substance to correspond.[33]

A man who can produce a well-made novel is one thing, a master craftsman altogether another, and profundity, even assuming that it is the major aspect of literature, is hardly the happiest category in which to exhibit James. The history of literature is likely to agree with the sobriety of Mr. Blackmur's recent remark [34] that "there has been too much written about James, much of it exaggerated, much of it perverse, much of it inflated, often as much blind by ignorance or fashion as by long study and great love."

What then is a reasonable assessment of James?

All writers but those of the first rank have a novice period in which they use, because they have still to grow beyond them, the standard novel-clichés of their day, and most writers never grow beyond these at all.* Anybody must be forgiven a first novel. And as it happens even the two great masters of our own day, Miss Compton-Burnett and Henry Green, have each a first novel hardly recognizable when compared with what they have

---

* By "novel-cliché" I mean not phrasing as such but a whole ambience. For example a recent novel opens like this:

> "Well, as I keep saying," said Janet Links, "I think psychoanalysis would help you."
> George Links stared at his wife with his habitual listless moodiness. He was trying to remember why he had married her in the first place.

This appears in every respect—the flat diction, the hackneyed rhythms, the dispiriting intellectual level of composition—to be the start of a medium-grade pedestrian whodunnit. Yet it is serious: *A Travelling Woman,* by John Wain.

written since. But James was unusually slow at finding his mature style, and, as my quotations from *The Bostonians* show, singularly uncritical of the literary jargon of his times. The influence of the French novel and of Turgeniev may well have helped retard him, in the sense that they were models yet not models for English. If I am right in calling his search for a style, as late as *The Bostonians,* a matter of anxiety, even of floundering, then his gradual development from statement to implication, and the mixed riches of his impressionist discoveries, simply came too late in life to be natural. It would be like learning a new language too late in life; one would always be showing off one's idioms. This would explain why there is so much surface embellishment rather than good clear English in James's later writing, so much verbal maquillage instead of the bodily change, so to speak, that distinguishes the later Yeats from the earlier. If moreover James was not a particularly impressive critic of literature—and most Jamesists concede this, grudgingly—then we should not expect the shortcomings in his performance on other people's work to be entirely absent from his assessments of his own. Mr. Blackmur might well have put it less absolutely today than he did in his introduction to the *Prefaces,* that "there has never been an author who so saw the need and had the ability to criticize specifically and at length his own work." [35] For then how does it happen that James didn't write and re-write *better?* Why has he left so much that the dedicated Jamesist must either be trained, or be congenitally dull enough, not to see? I have suggested that when something was not going well he knew it, though not always why, and rarely analyzed why; and though what he lacked for discovering the why, and correcting the what, may have been in part resoluteness, still he must somehow have been looking at the writing in some wrong way as well. For the *Prefaces* are self-exculpation and advertisement besides what they purport to be, and there is too much they do *not* say.

As James miscast Adam Verver for his role, so has James's role, it strikes me, been misplotted for him. Granted the beauty of the academic schemata, the moral fascinations and ecstacies of planning it, the glorious daubings of doctoral detail, why on earth not pick a character that fitted the part in the first place, instead of just James? For above all he seems to have lacked the professional self-discipline which is the very heart of the role that academic criticism assigns him. He wrote too much, and reflected on what he wrote far too little. He wasted his time and his talents on things he merely wanted celebrity from. He relied on plans, in the face of every kind of evidence of what planning did to him. To understand how far in professional discipline James fell short, one need only contrast his output with that of a really disciplined writer, Henry Green's: eight novels in the twenty-four-year period 1929–52, yet probably not a thousand words Green would wish or need to rewrite even in the earliest of them. Green is of course more gifted than James. But the point is how he has disciplined and *worked at* his gifts: the pauses between novels are not pauses but an intense and endless examination of his art, so that every novel has been something wholly and astonishingly new. In James, all is unconsidered paradox and confusion of the will—a constant self-exhortation to "dramatize, dramatize!" yet a devotion to a way of writing that slows the action to a crawl and inundates the plot with a bilge of irrelevances; an infatuation with mechanical melodrama and well-made boulevard play, yet an unwillingness to work out his *scènes à faire* to the full; over-anxiety about his audience, yet delusions of what it consisted of and blindness to what his lamentable anxiety implied; creativity confounded with the mere scrabble of industriousness; above all, the arrogance of a settled way.

NOTES

1. Herbert Read, *English Prose Style* (London, 1928), pp. 218–19.
2. Donald Sutherland, *Gertrude Stein* (New Haven, 1951), p. 21.
3. Introduction, *The American Novels and Stories of Henry James* (New York, 1947), p. vii.
4. Leon Edel, Introduction, *The Portrait of a Lady* (Modern Library, n.d.), p. 20.
5. Richard Blackmur, Introduction, *The Golden Bowl* (New York, 1962), p. ix.
6. Sutherland, p. 48.
7. Introduction, *The Art of the Novel* (New York, 1947), p. vii.
8. F. R. Leavis, *The Great Tradition* (New York, 1963), p. 129.
9. *Ibid.*, p. 128, footnote.
10. For non-Latinists, the line minus the variants means "wounded her soft face with his hands"; the variant *inmittens* suggests assault, the variant *inmites* means "rough." Latin stylistics make the contrast *molliaque inmites* (soft/rough) an automatic choice.
11. Edmund Wilson, "The Ambiguity of Henry James," in *The Triple Thinkers* (New York, 1948), p. 106.
12. I am bound to say that the evidence of his fiction lies all the other way. The characters that interest him the least are his men. How hard he often had to work to overcome this temperamental set and "make" them interesting is plain enough from the forced-draft prose he portrays them in, the laboring engine of invention balking again and again.

13. Leavis, p. 153.
14. *The Notebooks of Henry James* (New York, 1947), p. 47.
15. Quoted *ibid.*, p. 49.
16. Which is, unhappily, what occurred in *Pudd'nhead Wilson* and *Tom Sawyer Abroad*.
17. F. W. Dupee, *Henry James* (New York, 1956), p. 129. James's fumbling phrase is from Chap. 18.
18. P. 55.
19. Leavis, p. 126.
20. I am regrettably reminded of a remark of Maurice Green's: "I'm afraid Mr. —— has rather a bed-sitter type of mind." *The Cherwell*, 19 November 1927.
21. E. E. Cummings, *Collected Poems* (Harcourt, Brace, n.d.), #167.
22. Introduction, *The Golden Bowl*, p. xiv—where, when Mr. Blackmur describes Mr. Verver as a hedonist of a very high order, I take him rather to have been turning a phrase than seriously redefining, after immurement in the Princeton English Department, the heights of human enjoyment.
    Incidentally, the oppressive effect of Mr. Verver on even this most brilliantly alert of minds is shown by Mr. Blackmur's slip: "this little old man" is a mere forty-seven (Chap. 7).
23. Frederick C. Crews, *The Pooh Perplex* (New York, 1963), pp. 118–120.
24. 30 December 1804.
25. For example, Mr. Leavis's "the style involves for him, registers as prevailing *in* him, a kind of attention that doesn't favour his realizing his theme, in the whole or locally, as full-bodied life." *Op. cit.*, p. 168.
26. *Show,* August 1964, pp. 59 sqq.
27. For those whose nerves can stand it, the opening clause has 19 syllables with 5 stresses, the next has 22 with 5, the last 22 with 7, and the headlong cadenzas of the first two clauses are checked in the third, and slowed down for the period, by a pair of subordinate clauses the latter of which has just half the syllables of the former. Cicero himself might moreover have approved the *clausulae* in which the *incisa et membra* end—the first a hypercatalectic double anapest, the second a cretic and anapest, and the anapest-iamb-anapest of the third deftly disguised by the lack of any real stress in the iambus.
28. *The Golden Bowl*, Chap. 26.
29. Read, p. 147.
30. Introduction, *The Golden Bowl*, p. vi.
31. Leavis, p. 172.
32. F. O. Matthiessen, *Henry James, The Major Phase* (New York, 1963), p. xiii.
33. Leavis, p. 11. It is an unnoticed irony that James said the same of Meredith: "Of course there are pretty things, but for what they

are they come so much too dear, and so many of the profundities and tortuosities prove when threshed out to be only pretentious statements of the very simplest propositions." *The Letters of Henry James* (New York, 1920), I, p. 224.

34. *New York Review of Books,* 26 September 1964.
35. *The Art of the Novel,* p. vii.

The learned no

Do nothing, not just think it, all day long.
—Harriet Hall

If one could assume that Classicists, unlike the rest of the race of man, delighted in common sense, or took example by its incidence, one might see cause for hope in a recent attempt to reanimate the drooping splendors of the Greek and Latin literatures while there is still anybody this side of Elysium with enough education to read the languages they were written in. For like a thunderclap from a clear sky

τέρας ἧκε Κρόνου πάϊς [1]

—a perfectly genuine Oxford Classics don has tried to look at the Classical literatures as if literature were what they in fact might be and he a literary critic; and for all I can tell the golden age is upon us.

For here is the promising second volume of *Critical Essays on Roman Literature,* a collection by several hands edited by J. P. Sullivan of Lincoln College.[2] The first volume, in 1962, was on the elegiac poets and Horace; this is on the Roman satirists; the explicit purpose in both is literary, "informed and serious discussion among professional students of the Classics, which is then [to be] reflected in teaching." [3] And if professional Classicists should once again, after a century or so, begin looking at what is spread on the page before them, instead of rummaging through it for Teutonic quantifications, perhaps they might indeed be brought to decide that a decent sense of their heritage required that they preserve it, and teach it once more with the literacy and the sophistication it calls for.

And contend for its survival. It is still barely a lifetime ago that preparatory schools taught Greek and Latin: the colleges made them. But in another lifetime, as things go now, there will not even be anybody who can read Homer. One would have expected our steady losses of students and departmental prestige to have goaded us into action decades ago, even if the Classics' loss of pride of place did not. Instead, there has merely been a steady disappearance of people who find such losses culturally appalling. It is this that Mr. Sullivan is in hopes of putting a stop to.

Now, to the man in the street (and to his offspring) what has been wrong with the Classics is simple enough, namely the way we persist in teaching the languages themselves. And why should he think otherwise? No schoolchild goes on with them long enough to find out what lies beyond the language phase anyhow, or indeed whether there is much of anything beyond for him to find. The pedagogic fiasco is of course not even half the story. Yet in his meat-headed way the man in the street is perfectly right about our methodology, and one has accordingly to look into his complaints before proceeding to the fundamental diagnosis.

2

Latin has a singularly straightforward grammar, and is in many ways much the easiest of the Indo-European languages to learn.[4] Against their arsenals of irregular verbs, all that Latin can muster is *sum-possum, volo-nolo-malo, do, eo, fero,* and *fio*—and how irregular are they? Or again, compare the baroque extravagances of the Romance subjunctive or the Russian numeral to the clockwork of Latin syntax, a syntax moreover for all practical purposes point for point our own. Add to this, that Latin is almost wholly undistorted by idioms, that its working vocabulary is small, and that its reading-matter, with rare exceptions like Persius, could hardly be more literal-minded, and one would have thought it a teaching topic that even an education-major might be up to.

But upon this simplest of linguistic bases there has for well over a century been spread for exhibit the most hair-raising grammatical taxonomy in the history of human perverseness—synecdochical accusatives, imperfects of dephlogisticated surprise, subjunctives of discontinuous contingent speculation, and more subdimidiations of the ablative than a Thomist could crowd onto the point of a medieval needle. No one would object if the stuff had been kept in the fatherland of its invention, where *Privatdozenten* might pronounce these resounding names with self-gratulation and patriotic pride, yet do no general harm. But if what Heaven had had in view was the abatement of folly, it would not have created the mind of man; and our grandfathers imported the German fashion for confections along with the German doctorate that inspired them. Thus began what even in our children's lifetime may not be ended,[5] the long madness of dosing out Latin to generations of cringing little boys as the most complex, Delphic, exception-ridden, and impenetrable tongue since Babel.

So deep into the grain is this pattern stamped that even the modern Deweymen's systems of escaping from it bear, in reverse, the grim marks of what they fancy they have escaped from. For all I know, many Classicists too still think that philology must somehow have been as real a part of what went on in a Roman writer's mind as his language itself. There are three general types of Latin primer on the market today, or on what is left of the market, but their methods of wooing the beginner differ only in their different ways of affronting his intelligence.

The traditional primer set out with the first declension, or something of the sort, and proceeded, quite at random, to pile up chapter after chapter until everything in Bennett had been paraphrased in detail. The structureless confusion of its author's mind—"mind" is hardly the word, but one must call it something—left even the brightest beginner with little more coherent notion of Latin than the vistas of pedagogical millinery the book set before his eyes. This called, in time, for reform. But to this reform, unhappily, our colleges of education brought their unteachable conviction that the way to cure you of folly is to counter-infect you with a still greater foolishness, their own. We had therefore a cycle of beginning-Latin books that flitted off either into a nursery-school ambience of no grammar whatever or into some dream-grammar in which paradigms and constructions pretended not to be there at all. This naturally did not teach anybody anything; it merely led to children's concluding that Latin must be even harder than people said it was, or their teachers wouldn't have been at such pains to present it as easy. Nor was the new reading-matter an improvement either. If the traditional primer dumped its victims into Caesar and Cicero, who are unreadable, the educationist replaced them with *fabulae, faciles* to the point of idiocy, which nobody but an educationist is dull-witted enough to read. Meantime Andover and Exeter bade Latin farewell in a cultured salesman's tones, and my own alma mater now accepts freshmen with no foreign language beyond two years of California-highschool Spanish, a requirement so debased that even a computer can learn it.

And so we arrive at the reform of reform, an Hegelian process of re-immersing oneself in one's original bog, but only hip-deep. Our Classics faculties are, however, often in the grip of our old guard still, so that any serious reformer, from mere political common sense, must himself adopt the same heavy-paced funambulation as they employ in place of mother wit. On the one hand therefore Latin appears once more to be an inflected language; on the other, the brains of schoolchildren are to be soothed, or obtunded, rather than encouraged to function, so we expunge as well as expound, and babble o' green language arts and speech-behavior as if we knew no more what we were doing than they.

3

Even the man in the street knows better. And yet his diagnosis of what is mistaken in our pedagogy misses what is in fact the most mistaken. What is wrong is another category of nonsense altogether: we have simply ceased to deal with our *litterae humaniores* as if we were the humanists we pretend to be.

First: the majority of us are not interested in the Classical literatures *qua* literature at all, but have taken to Greek and Latin because we have "scholarly" minds, which is to say, we like to fiddle with rebuses. Young men become dons for various ill-weighed and exotic reasons, some no doubt merely because they were marked donnish from the womb. But few are those, in any discipline, who teach literature because they love literature and understand it. Of most Classics men it is safe to infer, from their behavior, that they are Classics men because they delight in the sheltered rearrangement of archaeological minutiae. This has value. But its value is greater for other disciplines than ours, and all the brilliant excavations on Crete or at Pylos are useless to annotate

> *vixere fortes ante Agamemnona*
> *multi, sed omnes illacrimabiles*
> *urgentur, ignotique longâ*
> *nocte, carent quia vate sacro.*[6]

And second: of that negligible minority of us for whom literature does come first, almost none are competent to teach literature as literature. Classics men are hired, like anybody else, less for their abilities than for their incidence; what wonder then if they lack the sensibilities which only a biassed Heaven can bestow, and bestows on few? Add to this, that those few must, as things stand, be trained rather as positivists than as humanists, and the wonder is that anything but a ghetto of erudition is left to us at all.

For Classics men have long eschewed—longer perhaps than anybody—the primary discrimination between what is worth reading and what is rubbish. This has made perhaps less difference in Greek, which is a splendid literature like English or French. But Latin is a very different matter, a great part of it a mere hodge-podge of dreary tracts and legal bombast, and one has constantly to weigh up and assess. But suppose one cannot? *Mens sibi conscia recti* (which I offer as a nobler expression than "human vanity") forbids our admitting to incompetence in the very literature we are professors and purveyors of; and we have therefore been driven to dissemble our circumspection, and justify our doing nothing, by propounding learned scruples whether there is even anything we should do.

> Is criticism of the sort envisaged possible at all? . . . After all, both the languages with which we deal are *dead.* . . . How can we recover the inwardness which would allow us to feel as subtly as in our own . . . the *tone* of a given poem?

That is Mr. Sullivan; [7] and I will add: alas. Moreover, Mr. Lee of St. John's (Cantab.), forgetting that he has just said of Ovid that Latin "had never *sung* quite like this before," bears his distant countryman out:

> how far can we get inside poetry in a foreign language and, what is more, a dead one whose spoken rhythms are entirely unknown to us, whose spoken vocabulary is only patchily known, and whose poets have survived in exiguous proportion and sometimes by pure chance? [8]

What staggers the mind about these exercises in the rhetoric of diffidence is not that they can be shown to be nonsense, but that anyone should ever have mistaken them for anything else. Even at the simplest *ad hominem* level, no educated man can in fact do other than make judgments of a literary order, "inside" and valid for himself, on every line he reads as he reads it: that is simply how the educated mind works. There may be reason to be daunted by the prospect of having one's *ad hoc* assessments made public. But this does not mean that one does not make them; and in the marshalling of anagogic scruples I have just quoted, our English colleagues are merely engaged in denying having done what they are doing, by pretending it is not something one can do.

But on an intellectually more respectable level: Why should one assume that Augustan or Elizabethan English are not dead languages too, just because they somewhat resemble our mother tongue? In what sense can Mr. Sullivan "recover the inwardness" of

> *They fle from me that sometyme did me seke*
> *Stalking with naked fote in my chambre*

or Mr. Lee tell whether its spoken rhythm was iambic and had five beats or, like Wiat's Italian models, was syllabic and stressed differently altogether? Even in

> *Can storied urn or animated bust,*

what Gray meant by "animated" is plainly not what it now means to us.

Or, put the other way round, can I in the 1960's judge only what's written in the 1960's in my own tongue, or will an extra language and century be conceded for an act of literary judgment on, say, Jules Laforgue, b. 1860? Then what about a second century, for Constant, b. 1767, or Chateaubriand, b. 1768? And since Mr. Eliot's fashionable old foot is in the door, how refuse Italian and a half-millennium further, for Dante, b. 1265? At this point one hears a ghostly Constantian *Et bientôt l'adorable distraite, tout éplorée, n'avait plus rien à me refuser,* and we might as well be back in the Latin of Ovid, b. 17 April 43 B.C., which was two thousand years ago no farther from the 1960's than 17 April 1958.

Or again: even accepting the "inside/inwardness" recipe as if it were the whole instead of a mere part of the critical act, how can two such accomplished Latinists protest that they are deaf to the changing modulations of the language's "tone"? The mode of Ovid's *Amores* III, 3, for example,

> *esse deos i crede—fidem iurata fefellit*
> *at facies illi quae fuit ante manet,*

is approximately that of our cavalier poets, though Marlowe a century earlier did an adequate version:

> *What, are there Gods? her selfe she hath forswore,*
> *And yet remaines the face she had before.*

Ovid's lightness, which Marlowe doesn't catch, is due to a manipulation of *f, d,* and *t,* and a predominance of short *a, e,* and *i* (Marlowe's rhymes in *-ore* are a tonal mistake). Now hear the sibilants and vowels of *Amores* III, 14:

> *non ego ne pecces, cum sis formosa, recuso,*
> *sed ne sit misero scire necesse mihi.*

The heaviness, the dolor, the international lamentation of long vowels appear in Marlowe in what I take to be an Elizabethan equivalence:

> *Seeing thou art faire, I barre not thy false playing,*
> *But let not me poore soule know of thy straying.*

Two millennia and a dead language are not the point: certain stimuli are universal—sense and, above all, sound. The thoughts that hurt the English yeoman, the vowels that move him, they are there.

For that matter, if we cannot judge a piece of Latin literature in the original, why read it in the original either? If the legerdemain of *Heroides* 13,

mittit, et optat amans, quo mittitur, ire, salutem

is beyond my sensibility, let me content myself with

Your sweetie sends best wishes
Where she'd like to go herself.

It may of course be that Mr. Sullivan's diffidence is merely a polite expression of his doubts whether our colleagues can exercise literary judgment even in a language they do "feel subtly" in, their own. For here, the evidence of our feeling for words, a good rough-and-ready diagnostic, lies all on the side of doubt. One has only to look at a real Classicist's translations:

All, all in dishonour thou tellest it, woe is me! And for that dishonouring she shall pay her punishment: by the will of the Gods, by the will of my hands: Oh, let me but slay, and then perish! [9]

Here is a man dealing (one gathers from the context) with literature; except that literature, God knows, it is not. It reads rather like a paraphrase of something, for a kind of textbook meaning indisputably filters through the gibberish. But what could it be a paraphrase *of*? The style offers no clue. Indeed what language can we suppose this most celebrated Regius Professor of Greek fancied he was expressing himself in? Doubtless his mother tongue, though that was Australian; yet the result is no more either subtle or a feeling than the translators' choctaw that strained the good manners of Msgr. Knox.[10] We may no longer take pattern after the dreadful apparitions of our past, such pellmell on Ossian as Morshead's *Oresteia* or Starkie's Aristophanes, nor does today's average translation deserve Tyrrell's comment on Browning's, that you had to consult the Greek to see what the English meant. But Butler's Propertius is still with us, imaginary ethical datives and all; and a recent symposium [11] led by two of Mr. Sullivan's own colleagues, highly talented writers themselves, makes it plain that the Drydens are as non-existent as ever and the Robert Fitzgeralds hardly commoner. No one expects the ordinary Classics man to outwrite his great originals, with things like

> *Look round the Habitable World, how few*
> *Know their own Good; or knowing it, pursue.*

But one does expect him to "feel subtly" enough to see how and why this improves on

> *Omnibus in terris, quae sunt a Gadibus usque*
> *Auroram et Gangen, pauci dinoscere possunt . . .*

Instead, what we find, and find everywhere, is a scene that would be ludicrous if it were not a cultural catastrophe: the Classics man hopelessly purveying what he insists are two great literatures, to a public that has only to open his own translations of them to see that he is a liar.

4

But Mr. Sullivan is of course not really arguing that we must beware of bringing to languages beyond our critical sensibility a critical sensibility that we do not possess; and perhaps the fairest way of seeing what is wrong is by considering a specific case, the greatest among the Latin poets that his two volumes have dealt with, Ovid.

Ovid was in all likelihood a genius of the order of Mozart or Sir Christopher Wren. Like them, he lived in a world where manners had achieved what balance they can between the elegances and the anarchy of the senses. In particular like them, he seems never to have been at a loss creatively: not just that he was wonderfully prolific but that he was endlessly inventive and resourceful, with a fertility of wit and a polished mastery of language that were the stylistic climax of his time. Finally, as with Mozart and Wren, there lay behind the urbanity of Ovid's surface a powerful and original intelligence: the three are as one in taking the mere material of current mode and wholly transforming it.

The *Amores* for example are in form just the upper-class urban love-poetry of the day; but in Ovid two things are entirely new. First, there is his fascinated analysis of the degrees and modulations of sexual jealousy, all the way from the *non ego ne pecces* I have just quoted to the light-hearted elegance of

aquilamque in te taurumque timebam.[12]

And second, an insight of a depth and humanity rare in any era and as good as unexampled in antiquity: where his contemporaries wrote girls into their poetry as a kind of charming thematic decoration, Ovid saw girls as girls, and, what is extraordinary in a Mediterranean male, with affection. It is this warm insight into what he was *really* writing about that makes the *Ars Amatoria* less a handbook on love-making than a kind of pre-Renaissance treatise on manners, a *De Cultu,* and it is characteristic that Book III is addressed not to the marauding male but to young women, and that the tacit ideal throughout is hardly seduction so much as what one might today call sexual courtesy.

The *Heroides* in particular are something entirely new. They are in form a collection of verse letters from various heroines of mythology to mythological lovers who have abandoned them, plus a set of what have come to be known as "the double epistles," such as Paris's letter persuading Helen to run off with him to Troy and her reply. Yet "form" misses the point completely, because the form that Classicists fancy they see is the wrong one. This reply of Helen's happens to be one of the key masterpieces of European literature: its mere 268 lines contain in embryo everything that has, since, developed into the novel of dissected motivations that is one of our glories, from *La Princesse de Clèves, Manon Lescaut,* and *Les Liaisons Dangereuses,* to Stendhal and Proust. And all this mastery while Ovid was still a young man.

I have yet to discover a Classicist who even suspects it. "Ovid died, for at least the third time, in the nineteenth century, and was buried deep under mountains of disparaging comment," wrote T. F. Higham in an almost unique appreciation a generation ago,[13] and Mr.

Wilkinson has very justly laid much of the blame on the Romantic critics'

> insistence on the sharp distinction between what is poetry and what is merely verse, and their biographical approach to literature. Sometimes it is expressed by saying that [Ovid] has no heart [Mackail]. . . . More often it is a soul he is said to lack. . . . He is not 'sublime'; nor is he 'profound' [Arnold; Palgrave].[14]

These rushlights of the nineteenth-century mind are still held to provide illumination in the twentieth. *"Ovide fut un grand poète . . . dans la demi-poésie,"* began a paper read at Ovid's own bi-millenary, yet not a voice was raised in impeachment. Higham's point that Ovid's standards were not moral but aesthetic went unheeded in 1934 and remains unheeded—in 1964 a Professor Otis could announce in a book on Vergil, to the general applause, that "the Romans are above *art* because they have character," [15] and Higham might have saved his breath.

The aesthetic befuddlement involved in this sort of nonsense has been analyzed by Mr. Allen of Colby College with a clear-headedness rare in a Classics man:

> critics have often looked for proof of sincerity not chiefly in the artistic illusion created by the poem itself but rather in the relation existing between the poem and the external facts of the poet's life. . . . Since the poetry of Ovid is deliberately 'conventional,' many critics deny him sincerity, and as a corollary assume that his poetry is pure fancy supported neither by true feeling nor true experience.[16]

But there is also that additional cause for critical astigmatism about Ovid, "the age-long puritan deprecation of his attitude to sexual morality." [17] And beyond doubt a century that sees nothing edifying in that faintly smiling mutual sophistication with which man and woman touch each other's hearts in Congreve (*ridenti mollia ride*) will also evidently deplore Paris's saying things like

> *ut te nec mea vox nec te meus incitet ardor,*
>   *cogimur ipsius commoditate viri,*[18]

and the whole dazzling feminine comedy of Helen's reply. Yet I suggest that it is less a moral disapprobation as such in the critics than a kind of moral illiteracy. It was not just that Ovid, on love and above all on women, knew what he was talking about and says so, but that his Victorian critics, in all honesty, had trouble with the whole ambience of his world,

> which, though for the time it was living and actual, is as unreal to us as that of the Restoration dramatists.[19]

Mackail's hard head and relative lack of Victorian self-deception is what one likes to think Balliol under Jowett turned out invariably. But the Victorians' general experience of life was too defective to let even the most astute of them see that the *Amores, Heroides,* and *Ars Amatoria* form as masterly a "study" of one aspect of the human heart as, for instance, the *Antigone* is of another.[20] Ovid's Victorian critics were no more up to Ovid than to, say, Choderlos de Laclos. They accordingly mistook his stylization of perfectly normal human behavior for distortion, even misrepresentation; and having confounded the fictitious and the artificial, they called shallow what they wanted the worldly knowledge to recognize as profound.

One makes allowance for this sort of thing from an era

When reigned serene, in an eternal Sunday,
That Methodist Astraea, Mrs. Grundy.

But how excuse it today in volumes proposed to us as serious literary reassessment? If Ovid is not to have credit for inventing the novelist's form, at least one expects something on the humane maturities of his insight, or his Mozartian mastery of the whole dizzying orchestration of the female heart. Instead, the evergreen simplicity with which, in 1925, Rand [21] spoke of Ovid's "undeniable interest, and perhaps some experience, in intrigue," is echoed by Mr. Wilkinson three decades later: "No doubt he was not without amorous experience, but reading and talk could have given him most of the motives that occur." [22] What simulacra do Classicists consort with in the belief that they are consorting with women, to be so unable to distinguish, by the mere ripple of his accent upon the ear, the happy addict of the delicious original?

Small wonder, then, that from incomprehensions so basic and so built-in there should issue forth, on almost every particularity of Ovid's art, such wild and such erratic misappraisal of what is right there under everybody's eyes. Even the Englishman's Honour Mods training doesn't make his critical findings more reliable. A lecture that Robinson Ellis delivered on 11 June 1912 was mostly about manuscript readings; but when he found time to insert his considered literary opinion that

> tender feeling combined with lofty imagination . . . seems to exist in the *Amores* in a higher degree than in any other work of Ovid,

what he turns out to be talking about (I am not making this up) was an aubade so light that Fragonard could have painted the illustrations, and elegies on the respective deaths of a poet and a parrot. Nor is the Honour Mods' understanding better of how Ovid wrote: a Professor Grant takes as quite literally indispensable to the act of composition a Brontë's eye in a fine frenzy rolling, and complains that Ovid

> regards [his heroines'] psychological performances observantly and sympathetically, yet in writing of their passion he himself remains wholly dispassionate.[23]

Imagine Flaubert's comment. Rand's theory of composition was no nearer common sense: Ovid

> invents a mistress and a world of escapades, partly to give his fancy rein and partly to indulge in sprightly fantasies.[24]

What under Heaven went *on* in the mind of a man who could think that this described the same act of creation that has produced Manon, Clarissa, the Présidente de Tourvelle, Elizabeth Bennet, Mme. de Rênal, Anna Karenina, Charlotte Stant, Albertine?

But the finest flower of Ovidian uncriticism is German. "Ovid's modern editors," wrote Housman in 1897, "have been unfortunately distinguished by the very least Ovidian qualities in the world: an instinctive dislike for simplicity and a warm affection for the hispid." [25] Housman's topic at the time was the text of Ovid, and his derision was addressed to Merkel, Riese, and Ehwald; but he might with prophetic genius have been describing the current standard work on Ovid, the 1945 Sather Lectures, and its author Hermann Fraenkel. *Aliter,* we are told, *dis saepe videtur:* Heaven's views are seldom ours, and we are to bow our heads and chafe not; and why Professor Fraenkel proposed himself to expound the Mediterranean elegances of Ovid I cannot tell. But if you wish to blame the gropings of professorial critics today upon the professorial critics their youth was formed by—a point I made to start with—then here, ready to your hand, is the instance for all your argument.

Vox faucibus haeret, but I shall have to quote: no one will otherwise believe what the Classical establishment has not only swallowed but, for twenty ruminating years, mistaken for food.

There is, first, the amateur critic's happy irrelevance, like the comment on *Amores* III, 4,

> *si qua metu dempto casta est, ea denique casta est;*
> *quae, quia non liceat, non facit, illa facit*

that it "seems strangely to anticipate" the Sermon on the Mount.[26] Matthew 5:28 has, alas, been anticipated

from the day the first dawdling girl *limis subrisit ocellis,*
and among other things Professor Fraenkel overlooked
is that it was Athenian law.[27] There is the wild plunge
into sheer mirage:

> The striking phrase *sua sidera servat* [*Amores* I, 13, 11]
> establishes a personal bond between the sailor and
> "his" stars. I do not know whether anywhere else the
> stars "of" a particular person are mentioned.[28]

The lilies "of" some particular roses had escaped his
attention in *Amores* II, 5, 37, to go no farther; but as
any English schoolboy could tell him, *sua* is there for
purely metrical reasons. There is what might be digni-
fied by the term Wagnerian smog:

> *tunc ego me primum coepi sentire nocentem:*
> *sanguis erat lacrimae quas dabit illa meus.*[29]

> Experiences of this sort do not seem extraordinary to
> us. But it was an unheard-of novelty for the ancients
> that a person should no longer feel securely identical
> with his own self.[30]

—followed by two long notes on "fluid identity." There
is the amateur's teratological lack of proportion: five
solid pages on the aubade *Amores* I, 13, against a mere
twenty for all the other forty-eight *Amores* together.
There is ubiquitous naïveté: "Ovid is able to see everything with the eyes of the woman with whom he is in
love." [31] And overriding all is Professor Fraenkel's
learned disinclination to *look* at what he is dealing with
before he deals with it. Hear him on the *Amores:*

> The modern reader feels somewhat annoyed by the author's concentration on his main theme, and heaves a sigh of relief when once, by exception, he is permitted to visualize a concrete setting of rural scenery and to sympathize with the lover's deep attachment to his paternal soil.[32]

What is back of this preposterous sentence is, I suggest, not so much frivolousness as confusion, and I should set beside it for diagnostic comparison the *rudis indigestaque moles* of critical refuse in sentences like

> The subject [a lovers' quarrel] does not particularly appeal to our taste; but if for the time being we set aside our legitimate objections, we shall appreciate the fine qualities of the poem and the genuine sentiment behind it.[33]

It is useless to translate this back into German in the expectation that its confusions will vanish when expressed in a language where confusion is not just second nature but a necessity if one is to make oneself understood. Nor is this the percussive blankness of

> *A stolid nation, far renowned and long*
> *For judging of what's what, and judging wrong.*

No, it is here among us too, and Professor Fraenkel's is only an elderly, styleless, and uncircumspect way of saying what modern Classicists think and say also—say in far finer language, it is true, and with every magisterial ambiguity that an anxious intellectualism can devise; but the long training, the methodology, the scruples of our discipline, the disheartening ideas, are the same. Heaven, I conclude, with the high purpose that is its wont, set Professor Fraenkel before our eyes for a *monstrum,* and here, in one volume, as paradigm and guidance for all, has been compendiously assembled every critical vagary possible to the mind of professorial man.

5

Nevertheless it is more instructive to compare the Ovid chapter in Mr. Sullivan's book with what Mackail wrote seventy years ago.

Mackail was a driving, highly trained, and shrewdly sophisticated Scot; he came up to Balliol in 1878 (the same year as Lord Curzon, Sidney Lee, and J. St. L. Strachey); his tutors were Evelyn Abbott and Nettleship; he won the Hereford, Ireland, Craven, and Derby Scholarships and the English Verse Prize, took Firsts in Honour Mods and Greats, and became a Fellow of Balliol, merely as a start to his career.[34] What he had to say, *aetate suâ* 35, on Ovid, one can take as the best, the considered, opinion of his time:

> the same sure and swift touch is applied to widely diverse forms and moods. Ovid was a trained rhetorician and an accomplished man of the world before he began to write poetry; that, in spite of his worldliness and his glittering rhetoric, he has so much of feeling and charm, is the highest proof of his real greatness as a poet.
> But this feeling and charm are the growth of more

mature years. In his early poetry there is no passion and little sentiment. He writes of love, but never as a lover; nor, with all his quickness of insight and adroitness of impersonation, does he ever catch the lover's tone, [although we] know him from other sources to have been a man of really warm and tender feeling.[35]

This is insularity in its offshore-island perfection. Whether Jowett did or did not invent the Establishment can be debated; but he staffed it, and Mackail was as much a part of it culturally as Curzon and Strachey politically. Mackail had, to make him a critic, nearly every perception that Heaven, or astuteness that Jowett, could bestow: but of the three of them only Heaven really understood what went on all those leagues away across the Channel. One recalls the description of a Continental honeymoon by a later Balliol wife, the Hon. Mrs. Peter Rodd: abroad was hell. When therefore Ovid writes in *Amores* I, 4,

> *multa miser timeo, quia feci multa proterve,*
> *exemplique metu torqueor ipse mei*

—"I turn cold thinking what he may do with you, for I have done it all myself, and I am wrung with the expert terror of my own example"—this does not constitute a lover's "tone" for the Establishment, so how could it have done for the Imperial Roman court or landed gentry either?—and your aesthetic view of Ovid took off from there.

The modern Englishman is less misled by absolutes, and his absolutes, like his confusions, are less uninternational. Here is Mr. Sullivan's Mr. Lee:

It is Ovid's intelligence that is individual, not his sensibility (if one can separate the two). His sensibility deals
in stock and generalized emotions of no great depth
or strength, but his intelligent invention manipulates
them and the themes related to them in a strongly individual way. The manipulation exercizes the reader's
mind and, up to a point, his feelings, and thereby pro-
vides him with enjoyment, and sometimes (though for
the twentieth-century reader this is pretty rare) with
a genuine insight into the human heart. . . . To stress
the intellectual genesis of Ovid's verse is not, of course,
to pass an adverse criticism, but merely another way
of saying that he is in the classical tradition.[36]

One has almost to say *quot verba tot vitia.* For example, *all* emotions are stock emotions: there being only
so many things mankind can feel, every one of them has
been catalogued since the dawn of articulate time.
Ovid's moreover happen to be the opposite of generalized, as the simplest sort of demonstration should make
clear. In Catullus 8 and *Amores* III, 11, the situations
described are the same: the outraged lover is not just
cocu for a few minutes now and then, like anybody, but
replaced. The requirements of sexual lamentation are
therefore identical, the exhortation *perfer! obdura!* is
natural to both; but the emotions are as individualized
as the poets themselves—Ovid quite clear about the real
bearing of the outrage, Catullus all childishness and self-
pity. What on earth is more "generalized" about one
than about the other? [37] Nor again does Ovid's being
objective or urbane or experienced mean that his verse
has "no great strength," or his topic, the ballet of sexual
selection, that he has "no great depth."

Nor can I make out what Mr. Lee means by his sensibility-intelligence-manipulation sentences. The first two of these nouns might conceivably stand for the unconscious and conscious sides of the creative act that results in a first draft, and "manipulate" for the process of revision; but it is hardly a description a working writer would recognize. Not only are sensibility and intelligence not separable as one writes, but the description would not fit even if they were. Mr. Lee's epistemology of enjoyment is still farther beyond me: we have not just a kind of Ciceronian *motûs animorum duplices sunt* but a third something too, "insights"— and which side of this wobbly aesthetic dichotomy do *they* come down on? And why do they not provide enjoyment? And finally, is there no better way of saying that Ovid is one of the master psychologists of literature than by claiming that the occasions when he can tell a contemporary Englishman something new about the human heart are "pretty rare"?

6

It seems likely that the mistake in all this is the misunderstanding about style, not just Ovid's style but style in general. The common notion of what constitutes poetic style is still soggy with the remnants of nineteenth-century taste. As it has been extremely well put by Mr. Tillotson (another Balliol man, but without Mackail's spiritual disadvantages), readers are

> brought up to expect poetry to be written in a certain
> way, its words to be chosen in accordance with certain

principles. They know what Wordsworth said about Pope before they read Pope. And this means that when they read Pope and other eighteenth-century poets, they apply the wrong criteria: criteria which are wrong because irrelevant.[38]

This means, and has long meant, that Classics men find the Vergilian moonlight in *Aeneid* VI, 270, pretty much what poetic moonlight *is*, whereas Ariadne's moonlit shore in *Heroides* 10, 17–18, is an attempt, they suppose, to produce the same effect on them, but, being "cold," is failing to. "Cold" is of course hardly the word; but the style is something Romantic critics neither liked nor understood. Indeed in their disapproval they sometimes hardly recognize it when it stares them in the face.

Now sleeps the crimson petal, now the white

may look poetic enough; but if I turn it, say,

iam rosa iamque petunt niveâ vice lilia somnos,

a Romantic critic is not unlikely to see it as what he calls "rhetoric." Conversely, he may well overlook the Romantic inspiration behind

May will come round again, as like as not,
And folly, like as not, along with May,

and call it "classical" because of chiasmus and Housman.
    It is this "blanket term 'rhetoric,' " as Mr. Lee has very justly said, "whose vagueness and pejorative implication has done Ovid a great deal of harm." [39] Among

other things it is not realized that "rhetoric" is often simply how a *motus animi* expresses itself. Helen cries tremulously to the importunate Paris,

> *at tu dissimula—nisi si desistere mavis—*
> *sed cur desistas?—dissimulare potes,*[40]

and the chiastic phrasing is the purest naturalism. The "vagueness" that Mr. Lee so justly rebukes has led to other sorts of critical oversight too, and indeed when Classicists write about Ovid's style they usually sound as if they thought

> *he could not ope*
> *His mouth, but out there flew a Trope.*

In practice, this is only a step from assuming that if you can analyze any given style into tropes, then tropes are, in effect, what that style is.

It happens that the most careful analysis of Ovid's style is the late W. H. D. Rouse's, in his *Demonstrations in Latin Elegiac Verse.*[41] Rouse was a master at Rugby, and this little book is one of the best ever written to teach schoolboys how to write acceptable elegiac couplets. It is based entirely on Ovid; the first forty-odd pages are in the main a minutely categorized thesaurus of hundreds of examples of how Ovidian style says this or that. Here is how Rouse lays the general topic out:

> In the first place, Elegiac Verse is mainly *Rhetorical.* It is concerned, that is to say, with *Antithesis* of word, phrase, and thought, not with logic, or the due subordination of one word to another. Secondly, it is *vivid;*

the ideas must be so presented that they call up a picture, or excite an emotion. Both these are just the qualities which make a popular speech successful.

I. A *Rhetorical* character is got by avoiding complex sentences, and by using *Antithesis, Parataxis,* and *Parenthesis.* . . .

II. *Vividness* is got by using (i) *Apostrophe,* (ii) *Exclamation,* (iii) *Question,* instead of a bald statement of fact. . . .

No one who has examined these specimens can fail to understand the essentially rhetorical character of Ovid's style; nor can anyone fail to admire the ingenuity which he shows in giving life to it. These devices are used in every possible combination, and in his best work the reader's interest never ceases. This, too, in spite of the triviality of his subjects.[42]

The book then proceeds with twenty-five beautifully detailed demonstrations of how elegiac couplets are made to "take shape out of chaos, why out of many possible renderings one is selected, what are the principles of the art"—from translations of Campion and Shakespeare down to a final tour de force, The House That Jack Built in elegiacs.[43]

Now, when one has learned how to knock out this sort of thing in this sort of fashion, it becomes hard not to feel that—somehow!—Ovid must have gone at it more or less in this way too. This feeling moreover is unlikely to be vulnerable to demonstrations of the equivalent mistake in one's own language, for example an assumption that Milton's mind went through the process

EYE-less	in GA-za	at the MILL	with SLAVES
trochee	*amphibrach*	*anapest*	*iamb*

and congratulated itself on the beauty of the counter-point.

And as I have suggested, the introduction of a cliché like "rhetoric" results in grotesque distortions of critical assessment. If the straightforward force of

quae facis, haec facito—tantum fecisse negato [44]

is called artificial on the grounds that repetition is a trope, but the lachrymose repetition of

Caeli, Lesbia nostra, Lesbia illa,
Illa Lesbia quam Catullus unam,[45]

is taken as a *cri du coeur* or the like, then the judgment as to which has "intensity" is exactly reversed, and the reputations of the two poets reversed with it. Even in minor details the "rhetoric" concept will misconstrue what is on the page. Ovid took a mild Hellenistic pleasure in things like

Castori Amyclaeo et Amyclaeo Polluci

probably very much as the French do in Racine's

La fille de Minos et de Pasiphaé,

and *Medeae Medea forem* is no more rhetorical than our "out-Herod Herod." But rhetoric they are called nevertheless. They must be: they are by Ovid.

All of which, it seems to me, it was the business of Mr. Sullivan's volume to deal with in severe detail.

7

Yet if Mr. Sullivan has not applied in quite the right court for the license of mortmain that we need, perhaps someone else may still, before it is too late, now take example if only by his application.

Melioribus Parcis we might expect so. But *melioribus Parcis* is a phrase invented by a people long resigned to settling for less and worse, and I see no evidence that a change in the behavior of Classicists is likely soon. It has yet to be shown that a confraternity dedicated to time-lag can be stricken overnight with common sense, or that positivists become humanists by the simple rustic act of staining their whiskers with henna. There is, again, the company we keep—the old guard, watching like Capitoline geese over the royalties of their textbooks and the spalling but still rectangular precepts of the *status quo*.[46] We even quail before college deans of admission, who quail before everybody else.

The ultimate reform may, for all I can tell, turn out to be what the education-mongers have had in mind all along, to root Greek and Latin out of the curriculum altogether. A professor of education is not concerned with what to teach but with how to teach it; after all, if his IQ were high enough to deal with what educated people are taught he would not be a professor of education. He therefore naturally comes to regard the content of a course as not merely of secondary but on the whole as of trivial importance, the logical methodology being to reduce the subject-matter to the 10-to-15 per cent of it that his mind can, with a little effort, grasp.

And if this means turning Homer into literature-for-use, a collection of cracker-mottoes and guides to conduct for happy children to look up solutions to human problems in, well, as one education-monger put it,

> such values . . . are common to the literatures of every tongue—and to both good and bad literature, by whatever standards we judge quality.[47]

Soap opera and Sophocles are one.

I need hardly say that the extirpation of Greek and Latin from our colleges would be childish. But collegiate administrative common sense is not something to count on. An ability to read Greek and Latin is, today, no doubt a luxury. But what is man's mind but a luxury, whether the ape knows it or not? And why under Heaven teach only what the very worst educated among us recommend? A case can even be made out for the Classics as a practical necessity:

> Cut off the Classics, and you cut off all the scholarly understanding of medieval history, of Roman law, and of the development of Christianity; you sever the romance languages from their source; you exclude all serious study of the major influences that have moulded English and French literature.[48]

And this is a mere selection from among practical necessities.

But the one great overriding reason is the unpractical one, the splendors of the Greek and Latin literatures in themselves. Who is going to convey the gorgeousness, the *beatissima rerum verborumque copia* of Pindar, but Pindar? How can you convey Clytemnestra's

ἔστιν θάλασσα, τίς δέ νιν κατασβέσει;

Sutherland's *The sea remains. Who shall exhaust the sea?* is much the best try, but the verb is untranslatable. How do you convey Vergil, or Horace? For that matter, how, short of a decent Classical education, can you even see what

aquilamque in te taurumque timebam

is about? And is all this simply to vanish forever?

—So much for a cheerless prospect, and by way of *numquamne reponam.*

NOTES

1. *Odyssey* 21, 415: "Jove's awful signal the Design foretold."
2. Though he now exhorts us *ex Ponto,* if I may thus describe that Getic desolation, the Γετῶν ἐρημία of Texas.
3. Vol. I, p. 3. An admirable example of what can be done is a school textbook just published, *Æstimanda* (Oxford, 1965), by two assistant masters at Harrow, M. G. Balme and M. S. Warman: 85 Latin and 27 Greek selections, with some English verse versions and literary parallels interspersed, the notes beautifully designed to make boys see more and more clearly (and thus eventually see first of all), the technique, the *art,* of what they read.
4. My own demonstration of this, upon the bodies of University of Colorado freshmen years ago, is summarized in *The Classical Journal,* xliv, pp. 293 sqq. Beginning Greek is almost as easy: (1) except for a stray theologian now and then, only bright students enroll, and (2) the complete grammar of the Attic sentence can be typed on the two sides of an 8½ x 11 sheet of paper. My smartest class of beginners read in the first year about half of Xenophon's *Memora-*

bilia, the entire first tetralogy of Plato (minus the philosophic detail in the *Phaedo*), about half of Plato's *Symposium,* and the *Clouds* of Aristophanes (minus the choruses, which I read to them).

5. A typical college-level symposium on what to do about teaching Latin is reported in *The Classical Journal,* xliv, pp. 106 sqq. It is with perfect seriousness proposed that case-statistics could be simplified under forty-two heads. Not only *risum tenuistis, amici,* but no one even rose to remark that erudition is not a form of knowledge.

6. Horace, *Odes* IV, 9: "There lived brave men before Agamemnon; multitudes, yet now not one mourned for; unknown, the long night shut down over them; unnamed by the inspiration of any bard."

7. Sullivan, vol. I, pp. 3–4.

8. *Ibid.,* p. 178.

9. Gilbert Murray, *The Classical Tradition in Poetry* (New York, 1957), p. 194.

10. Ronald Knox, *Trials of a Translator* (New York, 1949).

11. William Arrowsmith and Roger Shattuck, edd., *The Craft and Context of Translation* (Austin, Tex., 1961).

12. *Amores* I, 10, 7, which is untranslatable. For non-Classicists, the meaning is this: Ovid's current young woman was so delectable that he was in constant dread of Zeus's spotting her and carrying her off in one of his lecherous mythological disguises.

13. *Classical Quarterly,* 1934, pp. 105 sqq.

14. L. P. Wilkinson, *Ovid Recalled* (Cambridge, Eng., 1955), p. 443. The power and persistence of the dogma is shown by Mr. Wilkinson's unconsciously adopting it sometimes himself: "Nevertheless it is a fine poem, for once again sincerity breathes life into dry bones" (p. 79). Sincerity had nothing to do with it.
   The mistake is the more surprising in that Wilkinson's *Golden Latin Artistry* (Cambridge, 1963) is a sophisticated analysis of the part that sound and rhythm play in Latin prosody.

15. Quoted in *The Times Literary Supplement,* 2 July 1964, p. 567.

16. Archibald W. Allen in Sullivan, vol. I, p. 111.

17. Wilkinson, p. 442.

18. *Heroides* 16, 309–10: "As to the solicitations of my ardor, madam, suppose them not to stir in you a mutual flame, yet sure our manners are not so ill as to use his lordship's absence from your bed with the incivility of disinclination."

19. J. W. Mackail, *Latin Literature* (New York, 1897), p. 135.

20. Antigone had to be engaged to be married if only for the purposes of pity and terror; but why should an old pro like Sophocles *justify* this formal nubility, and confuse his audience, by sexing her up? A writer selects, from the infinity of what a woman can be, the few traits he needs for the work in hand, or that in particular delight him. The Hellenistic raving of Vergil's Dido is required by

epic convention as Vergil used it; the bitter end-of-summer passion of Ovid's Dido is wholly different, and in part different because his convention is different.

In passing, Ovid blandly corrected the older poet's inexperience. Vergil's Dido cries,

> *si quis mihi parvulus aulâ*
> *luderet Aeneas,*

which is wonderfully convincing if you haven't been there. But what *Ovid*'s Dido says is

> *forsitan et gravidam Dido, scelerate, relinquas!*

21. E. K. Rand, *Ovid and His Influence* (Boston, 1925), p. 11. Rand was misled by *Tristia* 2, 340, where he misunderstood his own mistranslation ("imaginary amours") of *falso movi pectus amore meum.* His misconceptions of literary tradition sometimes look like sheer typographical error: "Ovid's chief inspiration for something new in elegy came from Horace" (p. 11). On page 110 he has the grossest misstatement I can recall a Classicist to have set down: "Martial is a kind of proletarian Ovid."

22. P. 47. "Motives" here refers to the stock situations of New Comedy. But what have stock situations to do with it? *All* literature is stock situations.

23. Michael Grant, *Roman Literature* (Cambridge, 1954), p. 225.

    More disheartening still, because the book is a decent-minded—and contemporary—effort to look at Latin literature in a literary way, is Kenneth Quinn's *Latin Explorations* (London, 1963). Here is a cento judgment: "Ovid the poseur" (p. 266) with his "glib bravura" (p. 165) "nonchalantly abdicates the moral stature Catullus, Horace and Vergil had won for poetry," and lo, "the contact Roman poetry had established with the worth-while levels of intellectual and social life has been lost" (p. 135). The hopeless misconception of how genius operates might appear due to mere want of reflection—even forty-three years after *The Sacred Wood*—on what terms like *tradition* and *individual talent* imply; but when criticism juxtaposes the words "moral stature" and "Catullus," there is something more wildly wrong still, and with "worth-while" (of society under the principate!) history too is on the luckless edge of hilarity.

24. P. 11. A former professor of my own appeared to hold the view that Ovid was simply a further stage in the largely automated development of something called Subjective-Erotic Elegy.

    One would expect people dedicated to the chronologizing of nonsense to be among the first to see what is *original,* in Ovid or elsewhere. But *habet et sua castra Capella.*

25. *Classical Review,* 1897, p. 102.

26. (Berkeley, Cal.), p. 87. The couplet hardly deserves more than Marlowe's version:

> *Who, without feare, is chaste, is chast in sooth:*
> *Who, because meanes want, doeth not, she doth.*

27. τὸν βουλεύσαντα ἐν τῷ αὐτῷ ἐνέχεσθαι καὶ τὸν τῇ χειρὶ ἐργασάμενον, Andocides I, 94: "the man with intent is as liable as the perpetrator."
28. Fraenkel, p. 175.
29. *Amores* I, 7, 59–60: adding a couple of adjectives from the context, this means approximately

> *My heavy fault then first I understood:*
> *These hot tears she was weeping, 'twas my blood.*

30. Fraenkel, p. 21.
31. *Ibid.*, p. 22.
32. *Ibid.*, p. 185.
33. *Ibid.*, p. 18. Lovers of Professor Fraenkel may argue that he was here merely inventing a form of aesthetic differentiation which has since turned up in such respectable places as Martin Turnell's widely praised *The Novel in France:* "We may not find [*Les Liaisons Dangereuses*] particularly enjoyable or particularly edifying, but that it is a masterpiece we cannot doubt." (New York, 1958), p. 77. But Mr. Turnell is only saying he knows there is a difference between good literature and what he himself actually likes to read. This is hardly how the German mind works.
34. Curzon became something rather less exacting, a Fellow of All Souls.
35. P. 139.
36. In Sullivan, pp. 173–74.
37. Unless perhaps Mr. Lee takes Catullus's to be the genuine "lover's tone": his comment on p. 164 that Ovid's poem "is verse at a much lower level of intensity" looks sadly like the standard Romantic hallucination.

    What's really wanted is a neat little quantified dissertation assembling for our instruction all instances of literary childishness from Achilles's

    ἦ ποτ' Ἀχιλλῆος ποθὴ ἵξεται υἷας Ἀχαιῶν

    to its *volkstümlich* paraphrase

    > *I don't want to play in your yard,*
    > *I don't like you any more,*
    > *You'll be sorry when you see me*
    > *Sliding down our cellar door.*

    Instances of the pathetic fallacy might well be included:

    > *How can ye chaunt, ye little birds,*
    > *And I sae fu' o' care!*

38. Geoffrey Tillotson, *Augustan Poetic Diction* (London, 1964), p. 23.
39. In Sullivan, vol. I, p. 164.
40. *Heroides* 17, 151–52. A respectable couplet rendering is probably impossible, because the first and the final word must be either *feign* or *dissemble,* yet neither works—*dissemble* has no useful rhyme and is a feminine ending anyway, and *feign* seems to have nothing better than the forced and frigid *refrain.* The difficulty is made glaringly clear by what even Dryden was reduced to:

> *Dissemble you, what e'er you hear 'em say:*
> *To leave off loving were your better way;*
> *Yet if you will dissemble it, you may.*

This adds something that isn't there, leaves out something that is, and as good as mistranslates in general, for the literal meaning is "But for your part, dissemble—Unless if you'd rather stop?—But why should you stop?—You can dissemble." Which sounds no more like Ovid than a computer would.

41. (Oxford, 1899).
42. Pp. 1–2, 7, and 11.
43. As this is not something we do over here, and the book is out of print, I shall give an example: Mr. Rouse's deft handling of a couplet of Campion's.

> *Now winter nights enlarge*
> *The number of their hours*

WORDS. 'Winter': *hiemps, bruma; hiemalis, brumalis, glacialis.* 'Enlarge': *extendere se,* or the like.

FORM. This sentence should be broken up into two. We begin by saying, 'Now winter nights grow longer'; and then ask what can be done with the word 'hour'? What do the hours do? The hours of the night, or the 'dark hours,' shorten the day. This gives *hora diem* for the end of the pentameter, and *et tenebrosa* for its beginning. 'Shortens' must be paraphrased, since no metrical phrase at first occurs to the mind; but perhaps the student will think of Horace's *ver proterit aestas.* The idea of shortness will then be put into an adjective, and we make the phrase *brevem proterit . . . diem* for 'shortens.' Turning to the first line, we find no help in the simple translation *noctes se extendunt;* but substitute *tempora* for *se,* and the necessary dactyl is to hand. The rest is easy. We have only to place *tempora noctes* last, *glaciales* or *brumales* as a molossus before them, and we see that the phrase *iam ◡ ◡ extendunt* requires only a trochaic neuter adjective in elision to complete the line. This will be *longa,* intensifying the idea of the verb.

> Iam longa extendunt glaciales tempora noctes,
> et tenebrosa brevem proterit hora diem.

The effect of this may not be terribly Ovidian. There has of course to be padding, but filling up both lines with two adjectives, two nouns is a boring way to do it, and at a more advanced stage of instruction Rouse would do much better. Again, *proterit* seems to have been used to remind the schoolboy to make use of his reading—otherwise *prorogat* simplifies the task, an obvious skeleton being

> *iam* ◡ — *surrepit hiems, iam segnior* (or *tardior*) *annus*
> — ◡ ◡ *nocturnas prorogat usque moras.*

But the demonstration is masterly even if the couplet that results is not.

44. *Amores* III, 14, 15:
   What thou dost, do; swear only, 'twas not done.
45. Catullus 58:
   My Lesbia, the Lesbia, that one Lesbia whom Catullus . . .
46. The most brilliant essay on Classical style that I have ever read, Sutherland's "Dynamic and Aesthetic of the *Iliad*," was not even published in a Classical periodical—hence see the *Western Humanities Review*, Spring 1952, pp. 137–70.
47. *The Classical Journal, loc. cit.*
48. E. R. Dodds, presidential address, 7 April 1964: *Proceedings of the Classical Association*, vol. lxi.

   I might add: Cut off the Classics, and you have a full professor at the University of California beginning a letter to *Life* (2 July 1965, p. 25) with a sentence like "You will get brickbats for [an article on] graduate education, but here are enthusiastic kudos."

Che ti dice il Wilson?

Patrons are requested not to peer under the skirts of the chorus: they are only Cappadocian boys in disguise.

Everybody likes to support the axiom that, just as British justice never hangs an innocent man, so no piece of genuine literature is ever misassessed and overlooked in what is called the long run. This is handy and popular and furnishes anybody with a Natural Law against making up his mind: posterity will do that. But besides not explaining what happened to things like some hundred plays of Sophocles's that we do *not* have, such Arcadian simplicity has at least two Boeotian inconveniences. First, it lets into the canon—often so far in that we never really get them out—a great many writers who purvey not literature but brightly colored trash, like Carlyle and

Sir Walter Scott (and the process has been going on right before our eyes with Graham Greene and Henry Miller). And secondly, it dissembles something much worse: some of the most brilliant writing of our time has been so smoothly and universally ignored that it can hardly be said to exist as literature at all.

From the 1930's: *Yesterday's Burdens* by Robert M. Coates, one of the two or three original novels of the decade, disappeared overnight without a trace. From the 1940's: Glenway Wescott's masterpiece, *The Pilgrim Hawk,* in many ways the finest novella ever written by an American, fell almost as flat.[1] From the 1950's: Tennessee Williams's *The Roman Spring of Mrs. Stone,* a masterly adoption of the French novel form, and, as writing, much superior to his plays, was simply remaindered.

Now much of this was due to the critical incompetence that our axiom dissembles; and for that matter if things had had to be left to a Macedonian biologist like Aristotle where would Aeschylus be. But with Edmund Wilson's fiction—*I Thought of Daisy* (1929) and *Memoirs of Hecate County* (1946)—neglect has not been just a matter of carefree critical incapacity nor even, as for Williams, malice, but sometimes sheer childishness too. These two books comprise a novel, a long novella, and at least two short stories that are among the best of their kind in our literature; yet the most recent article I've seen on Wilson's fiction, by John Wain, contrived to fill eight solid columns in *The New Republic* [2] without mentioning *even the title* of one of them! Mr. Wain's intellectual plateau is typical: he complains that

Wilson "gives a slab of narrative and then talks about the significance of what he has told us"—an ignorance of Continental novel-technique that is hard to believe even in an Englishman. (This sort of thing, to borrow a phrase of Housman's,[3] creates in the reader "so strong a feeling of intellectual superiority as cannot be good for him.") Even the republications of *Daisy* in 1953 and more recently of the rewritten *Hecate County* have merely elaborated, not changed, the rhetoric of their dismissals.

So I shall start from scratch.

I Thought of Daisy is a five-part episode in a young man's life: back from the first world war, he sets out in Greenwich Village "to encounter for the millionth time the reality of experience"—here a kind of threshold-journey from college literature-courses to life, namely the arms (as in those male days was normal) of a decent quantity of young women. He is innocent of politics too:

> beyond publishing a few satiric verses in a radical magazine, I had never myself struck any blow in the war for humanity.

At a studio party in Part I he meets Daisy, an amiable, unaffected, and very pretty chorus-girl, who is living with a well-to-do dilettante; but he falls enchantedly in love, as literature in college had taught him to expect to do, with the famous young poetess, Rita. By Part II however he is trying to recover from Rita, who he decides is a tramp, and he finds Daisy, now on her own again, unexpectedly appetizing and wholesome. But tramps are hard to recover from, and by Part III his dilemma (what to put in the void Rita left) has reached the stage of demoralization, and Daisy, seen against what is now a nightmare background of Village humanity, no longer has the aspect of a remedy. (The void here can of course be read as what happens when "literature" is no longer enough but "life" has not yet taken over its hermeneutic function.) In Part IV however the antithetical recovery normal to youth begins: on a visit to a former professor named Grosbeake he rediscovers certain hereditary values, and presently decides that Daisy, now living a simple country life with another man, is somehow part of them. Finally, in Part V, he recuperates, thanks to a sort of working synthesis of Daisy's values with his own, her going to bed with him a kind of reinitiation back into humanity and the real world at last; and at the end he is pretty much himself again—not grown up yet, naturally, but ready for the next dialectical thrust of growth.

As this summary suggests, Wilson laid out a schema in some detail. The unnamed "I" of the story, he wrote in his foreword to the 1953 edition,

> is supposed to be a typical example of the American intellectuals of the twenties, who is always attempting to formulate an attitude toward life in the United States, and Daisy the American reality, who is always eluding his grasp.

This is worked out by schematic shifts in what is the main influence on the "I," different from part to part, and by providing at each turn a different subjective atmosphere. In the same way, Daisy herself, though a clear and consistent character for the reader, is for the protagonist a creature who changes with the place she occupies in his mood. Actually she too is in flux but this is not told the reader until the last scene. The modulations of the title-phrase serve as a key. At their first meeting, in Part I, "I thought of Daisy under the guise of a little blonde Venus caught in the net with Mars"—the most literary possible of allusions. In Part II, the first phrase on his lips is "I thought of Daisy" when he is free of Rita, "free to love another girl." The disintegrating mood of Part III is given in "I resolutely thought of Daisy" and the increasingly desperate "I tried to shift my thoughts to Daisy." In Part IV, the first glimpse of returning values, in Professor Grosbeake's household, "made me think of Daisy." Until finally the theme is resolved in Part V:

> I thought of Daisy under her different aspects . . . all so different from my present view of her, from our present reality . . . those phases of myself of which my successive conceptions of Daisy had been merely the reflections.

Now, a defeating fact is that nobody, in the third of a century since *Daisy* first appeared, seems to have performed the simple textbook act of asking what the title "means"—who this unnamed "I" is and what is all this thinking about Daisy anyhow? or why of all names something as unimpressive as Daisy?

Wilson's descriptive phrases are diagnostic enough—her "lovely American mouth," "her frank and charming grin," the "American thinness" of her hands; her profile too has a "fineness and purity of outline" transcending such random vulgarities as her very American accent. Then there is her location in the story ethically: if she is for example "adrift," it is her very sweetness and simplicity which cause the drifting. Such a namesake as Daisy Miller should then occasion no particular surprise, nor that other Daisy adrift in not unsimilar difficulties half a century later, Gatsby's Daisy Buchanan. The "I" is rather more than Wilson's 1953 foreword says: he is a particular rather than a typical young man of the era, and from a particular background,

> that world of our early years . . . where, for all its limitations, the ordinary contacts of life had been easier and more agreeable . . . [and] a common understanding had at least meant a mutual confidence

—a world, he goes on, of good manners, integrity, and cultivated intelligence, from those upper sections of society which have now "debased their distinction to luxury and made cowards of their leaders" by taking plutocracy for the national ideal: young gentlemen are trained for money-making instead of for the professions, as in Wilson's father's day, and one hears no more of "the honor of a family tradition . . . the disinterestedness of public service."

This is an Eastern upper-middle-class background; and in Part IV other components of the high-minded American tradition are assembled—the learned serenity of Professor Grosbeake makes "moral distinction attractive" and individualism admirable after the "horde of depersonalized masks" of Part III; even Daisy's country ménage with a temporary young man has still the old-fashioned virtues of leisure, order, dignity, and good manners. Daisy behaves like a well-brought-up child, and the pair pass the evenings reading Bulwer-Lytton aloud.

Why then the "I" thought of Daisy is plain. He has seen her as the common stuff of American life, the "reality" he is in principle after; but by Part V her smile has come to seem "unmistakably the smile of the young American girls of my boyhood," and in his mind she is not so much synthesized as confused with that vanished American decency and order whose values he is trying as an adult to reconstitute. His other guides to reality have turned out inadequate: Grosbeake specifically shuns ethical judgments (which no American can do without), and Rita's "foolish and shallow philosophy of living only for the moment" is not aberrant individualism but a rather messy solipsism.

> All that dignified mankind . . . [has] been built up through endurance and patience, through steadiness of purpose and good faith, through property well administered, through families standing together, through lovers true to their pledges!

The absoluteness of this statement, the unperceived irony of connecting it with Daisy, and the exclamation point with which it ends, remind the reader that this is still a very young man talking. And a young man is what the book is about—still juvenile (and literary) enough to exclaim "Let's run away together" as late as the next-to-last page. He is, in a word, very little nearer the certainties he solemnly tells us he has arrived at than when, at the end of Part I, in a wonderful *et ego in Arcadia* admixture of youth, Rita, and Poetry in the deepening radiance of summer dawn over Washington Square, he was certain that "something or other I had come for, I had found." The young woman spending the night in Part V is different, but it is in the same bedroom.

The urbanity, the detachment, and the wit of such a memorandum are as good as unique in a first novel, and so is the sheer condensed force of the writing. One brilliant example of this is the opening of Part II: in a mere ten pages the whole Rita-"I" affair is set out in the story of its heart-sick and wrangling final day, and the Manon theme has never been done more movingly or with a more distinguished economy. Again, the symbolic and thematic detail is at times almost spectacularly dense, as in the tissue of disintegration in Part III—disrupted family life, disrupted liaisons, disrupted lodgings (with Daisy connecting all categories by being in them all); the various levels of drunkenness, the descending levels and postures of love, ending in the introduction of two prostitutes; the dissolving neighborhood, the decomposing and intermingling social classes; the Dostoyevski theme and the disintegrations of the soul. There is a constant shower of wit, not just verbal, but the wit of incident, like Daisy's innocently acquiring sheet by sheet a letter which "I" had received from Professor Grosbeake and long treasured. There are a few vices of writing but they are very few, and what we have in the 1929 Wilson is a mature style of great surface brilliance and density, composed with notable care; predominantly intelligent, ironic, and witty though with rather high factors of imagery and color (he had just renounced formal poetry), with clarity perhaps the outstanding aim. And nearly everything wonderfully alive.

All of which it seems to me adds up, even at the professorial levels-of-meaning level, to one of the twenty novels of the decade—and I will amiably concede my difficulty in remembering all the other nineteen. Its virtues are in fact perfectly evident. Why did the critics not see them?

Well, they have not seen them yet; but in 1929 there was perhaps one special opacity that it is easy to overlook in 1967. In 1929 *Daisy* was an experimental novel, but it was not written in a way that *looked* experimental; and this is baffling. For how could anything so sober be avant-garde? It was even written in periodic sentences; they were even punctuated. Yet it was nevertheless a kind of novel the critical assemblage were as little used to as if it had been avant-garde: it was new—and how can one tell whether something is good or bad with nothing for comparison?

But *ad hoc* difficulties aside, it is easy to see what took place in 1929 because it is taking place still. To the ordinary reviewer's mind, Wilson is a critic; well then how can he write novels? so the thing to do is say he should stick to criticism, as Mr. Wain says he should do, where he is an inspiration and sits like Rhadamanthus for our instruction, discriminating among this fortnight's masterpieces. Then, on a somewhat higher level,

Wilson's fellow-critics can hardly be expected to concede that he's a novelist into the bargain, for where would that leave *them*? And finally, advanced intellectuals have to reject him, because what *is* avant-garde about him? he wasn't avant-garde even when he was young; Delmore Schwarz [4] said he was like "one of the sons of a hero of Henry James" anyhow; anyhow if he wanted anything as respectable as *Partisan Review* to take him seriously he should have stayed married to Miss McCarthy. Or swapped her for an equivalent. And look at his politics.

In 1929, however, Wilson was at *The New Republic* and hence capable of counteraction, so *Daisy* could not safely be panned. But it could be showered with nonsense instead; and sure enough, this unusually mature story about the process of maturing was promptly abused for being immature:

> One of the most promising and at the same time most annoying first novels which have [*sic*] lately been given us. When he has thoroughly digested his Proust, and recovered his equanimity, there is every reason to believe that he will give us a novel, or novels, worth cherishing—because entirely his own.

So the *Saturday Review of Literature*.[5] *The Nation* delayed its review for four months, and did not specifically endorse cherishability as a category of literary excellence, but otherwise said the same:

> If Mr. Wilson has freed his soul of a complex by this publication, then those who admire him in his more

familiar literary roles will have reason to be thankful that he "thought of Daisy." Not otherwise.[6]

It is instructive, though hardly improving, to observe how such journalistic nonsense in 1929 could set the tone for academic criticism nearly two decades later: in 1946, Professor Kazin, in *Partisan Review,* simply restates the last clause above with more surface sophistication:

> Mr. Wilson's subject is history, and in history the personal careers shape its meaning for him. . . . He [is] not really interested in fiction; only in using it to put a floor of imaginary detail under his historical commentary.[7]

It had not crossed Professor Kazin's mind that his final clause applies to any number of people he would never dream of applying it to as a rebuke. But more generally: had it never occurred to any of these fretting spirits that any writer worth the name has his own (which is never their) way of writing things? And that what they were fussing or snapping about, *inter alia* a texture of contemporary ideas woven into the narration, may quite simply *be* Wilson's way? And that accordingly a sensible critical attitude would be to accept this fact, and then see what follows?

Unfortunately, almost the only criticism of *Daisy* worth the name has been Wilson's own, in his 1953 foreword, that he adhered to his preliminary schema to the detriment of what might, once he was in it, have been more natural local developments in the story. I would add that there are also a few vices of style, largely due to the periodic sentence. This, Wilson does not invariably handle with the care it demands. In the opening paragraph of Part IV, for instance, the second sentence has 162 words, of which no fewer than 109 make up a parenthetical description inserted between the subject of the sentence and part of the predicate. Another form of periodic confusion appears in

> the beginning of a sonnet of which, the night before in my wakefulness, I had with obstinacy fixed in the target the accurate shafts of the end.

But these rare lapses (like the concluding anapests) are the accidents of momentary inattention.

Wilson's principal other fiction, *Memoirs of Hecate County,* is a collection of five short stories and that banned novella—in France it would be a full-length novel, and the form is as natural to Wilson as to a Frenchman—*The Princess with the Golden Hair.* And in this volume, the critical *clochards* inverted their earlier error: in *Daisy* they had not bothered to pick over the title for its meanings, but by 1946 Meaning was everybody's all, and they strode authoritatively about cross-tunneling *Hecate* for sign and symbol [8] that for the most part—in a book whose only theology is a kind of sardonic ex-Presbyterianism—are simply not there. "Hecate County" is a piece of loosely thematic real estate and a good title, with a bit of play on the word "witch," nothing more; the "theme of evil" which got so much critical wordage doesn't appear in *The Princess* at all.

This brilliant and moving naturalistic novella, which I propose to limit my remarks to, set off a puritanical earthquake all the way from Miss Kirkus ("isn't even good erotica") to the Supreme Court, which by a 4–4 decision unhappily refused to vacate the New York obscenity conviction. It toppled everybody between over too, with a couple of surprising exceptions: *Time* levelheadedly remarked that "such civilized writing and observation are rare in the U. S. nowadays," [9] and, in the *New York Times*,[10] Ralph Bates, less agog over sin than Americans, did an astute and laudatory review that even said what *The Princess* was about ("a love story"), something everybody else was apparently too undetumescent to be lucid on. It is particularly funny to listen to our liberal weeklies pretending *they* are not prudish and upset—Mr. Cowley in *The New Republic* [11] finds the weakness of *Hecate County* "essentially a lack . . . of animal faith," whatever that is, and Mrs. Trilling in *The Nation* [12] calls the stories "not . . . disturbing because they are daring, but . . . disturbing because of the breach they make between sensation and emotion." Many intellectual reviews did not notice the book at all.

The Princess with the Golden Hair is, like *I Thought of Daisy,* one cycle in an upper-class young man's progress toward the ultimate humaneness of age. During the long absence of his "regular girl" Jo (his counterpart socially and culturally) he has two love affairs outside his regular milieu—with Anna, a pretty little Ukrainian waitress from Brooklyn, and with Imogen (the Princess), a well-to-do young suburban beauty who, in place of chic, dresses in a sort of period-costume style and lives in a mock-Tudor decor (even cocktails are served in chalices). These affairs expand and humanize the young man's sensibility and very agreeably interrupt a dilettante book he was thinking of finishing; and the whole thing forms, as did *Daisy,* a descriptive dialectic of non-literary growth: "I now came to realize" and similar phrases are a thematic refrain.

This time however the form has a kind of reciprocating motion, the thesis Imogen answered by an Anna-antithesis which instead of synthesizing springs back as a newly formulated thesis toward Imogen again, and so back and forth to the end. Imogen enters as a fairy-tale dream of desire, "the fresh vision of boyhood" made tangible; but there being nothing very much to *do* on that level, Anna enters to satisfy the desire in reality. But this in turn extracts Imogen from hallucination; and since reality is one's bringing-up, the decent upper-middle-class "I" now begins to feel a moral responsibility about Imogen, wants to marry her and so on: from an immature ideal she becomes an ideal of love under conditions of order and good manners,

> a world in which the women made the basis of the families, gave their value to the proprieties and conventions.

And now this in turn he takes back to Anna, so that his feeling for her modulates into outright domesticity; he is in fact now in love with her, social gulf or no social gulf; and this new depth of feeling, recoiling, makes Imogen unsatisfactory. It is like going to bed with a Botticelli.

But analysis of this dissatisfaction not unnaturally brings on an uncertainty about his own motivations, which immediately oscillates back into his relations with Anna also. "How absurdly I had romanticized her, over-rated her!" he now exclaims; and this, helped along by an arbitrary hysterectomy, leads to his falling out of love with Anna and taking a now more experienced look at her; and so good-bye. And finally this "realism" acquired in leaving Anna has him saying good-bye to Imogen too, though the brusqueness of both adieux suggests that the inner decisions have still to be worked out, and may never be. So at last back comes Jo from California, his own kind of girl again, nice long legs and Chanel #5 and smart clothes and no sexual hesitancies—and the "I" is back once more at his book-that-never-gets-written, his pointless dilettante reconciliation of capitalist art with Marxist economics; and if he is also right back in the Hecate County he set out from, well, "it was the world, after all, that I belonged in."

Symbol and allegory can be read into this until one is professorially black in the face. But Wilson has focussed too intense a scrutiny on the human operation as such, and the characters are too naturalistically alive, to warrant concluding that we have anything here beyond a penetrating but simple modern-day tragedy. As Mr. Bates accurately said, the hero has "pitiable blindnesses and terrible imperfections [which] with uncommon precision . . . are chosen to reveal the meaning of his experience"—the story, in short, of a young man deeply loved by two extremely sweet young women, his tragedy being that he simply stays in his own world.

What we have, moreover, is a quite remarkable *prose* description of the course of love, written with singular virtuosity and concentration. I italicize "prose" because what the reviewers, like the rest of us, were used to—so used to that we in fact never expect anything else—is the lyric treatment, the incantation, of sex. An unusually gifted lyric poet of the *Hecate County* era—Spillane, say—could even treat it so lyrically that it disappeared altogether. Mr. Wilson, a plain and decent man, wanted to try treating it, for once, without stylistic raptures, if only to see whether a charming young creature like Anna would look as charming, and as humane, after exposure to mere prose. She does, and even Professor Kazin got around to admitting it; that is the measure of Wilson's art. And hence the uproar.

Hence too in part the neglect. We Americans have always had a terrible time with sex and evade its horrors when possible by maintaining that it is really just something that happens to other people. The fashionable fantasy was that it happens largely to people who can't do anything with it anyhow (children; homosexuals) or people whom it horrifies rather than gives pleasure to (all heterosexual characters in all serious novels except Mrs. Hutchins's). Any other view was intellectually plebeian; intellectually fashionable novels were therefore about children, gay boys, Southern males, city-university intellectuals, and slobs. Little-review fiction in particular was sexless. What Wilson had written in *The Princess* was therefore pornography; and since in 1946 pornography had not yet become an art-form, the only possible intellectual attitude toward him was to reject him (in many cases, rubbing one's hands). Besides, he belonged to the bathtub-gin generation, and in 1946 what one drank was an adequate little red wine. And this form of rejection still remains: the academic mind grinds exceeding fine, but it grinds slowly.

It is, also, a very much less resilient mind than it fancies. The ability to revise foolish opinions by which a dioristic Creator has marked us off from sheep is no commoner among one's academic colleagues than anywhere else; and the assessment of Wilson's fiction remains what it was two decades ago—which is to say, what it had remained for two decades before that. After all, one cannot in reason change one's mind halfway through one's dissertation; why then halfway through one's professorial career? One would merely lose academic face, and, with it, academic preferment; one's textbooks would become continually, and embarrassingly, obsolete. Rare indeed was the Princeton professor who not only changed his mind a couple of years ago about the history of the English novel but announced the change in print: "the great tradition [had] seemed to [him] to have come to an end . . . after 1928," and he "had pretty well given up"; but in 1964, stimulated by film versions of some of the best contemporary second-rank fiction, he had "begun to discover . . . that the English novel is on the track again." [13] He has now only to read the first-rank writers of the 1928–64 interval to discover that it may never have been off it.

But finally—"in the long run"—Wilson has been neglected because the academic eye does not really see *what* is on the page. The question a professor of literature asks, instead, takes the form: What is Wilson "saying"? And in that sense he is not saying much of anything. Even that glittering interpolation in Part III of *I Thought of Daisy*, on the mythology of literature, doesn't "say" in the professorial-insight sense. Nor does *I Thought of Daisy* say very much technically now: if in 1929 it was something that the critical apparatus of the time wasn't used to, in 1967 we are long past being used *or* unused to it, the technique of the novel having so to speak moved on. In any case 1929 happened to be the date of two novels of much more vigorous originality, Green's *Living* and Faulkner's *The Sound and the Fury*, and there followed such brilliant explorations of form and method as Coates's *Yesterday's Burdens* (1933), Beckett's *Murphy* (1938), and Green's *Party Going* (1939). To the specialist in the technique of the novel, *I Thought of Daisy* is likely to look like just the standard this-and-that about a young man; he is more or less in rut; there is more or less of some kind of literature-and-life nexus; and so forth. And what is *The Princess with the Golden Hair* but more of the same?—less literature and much more rut, but the same. Since therefore the oeuvre "says" nothing, what is there to say about *it*?

It can of course be abused for programmatic reasons, as Professor Hyman did (as nastily as he could) in *The Armed Vision*. Or again, now that *il mio dolce dottore* Freud has reanimated the biographical method that should have expired with the Romantic critics who foisted it upon us, one can win approbation by discussing what Wilson writes as what Wilson is:

the man wants to tell us something about himself, and
has made sure that he will not. The result is to reduce
the book [*Hecate County*] to a curiously covert kind
of commentary.

So said Professor Kazin, and he spoke for a confraternity
without number.

In principle there should be a lesson in all this. But
if Heaven had intended mankind to avoid arguing in a
circle, it would not have included *petitio principii* in
the nosegay of fallacies whose scent we find so heady and
so pervasive. *Die Fehler sind dazu da,* said Savielly Tartakover, *um gemacht zu werden.*

NOTES

1. It is now available in a Dell reprint, *Six Great Modern Short Novels.*
2. 12 January 1960. Mr. Wain mentions only the two un-stories *The Milhollands* (half a column) and *Mr. and Mrs. Blackburn* (six lines). The childishness of this is matched only by the editorial levity of printing it.
3. *Classical Review*, 1934, p. 139.
4. *Accent,* Spring 1942.
5. 23 November 1929.
6. 1 January 1930.
7. *Partisan Review,* 1946, pp. 375 sqq.
8. E.g., Professor Kazin saw the three women in *The Princess* as "representing . . . periods in time to which the narrator returns in dreams; not always waking dreams"; they "symbolize the alternate and negotiable levels of consciousness on which we live"; and so on.
9. 25 March 1946. Less of a surprise if one recalls that *Time* then had an editor who was literate, T. S. Matthews.
10. 31 March 1946.
11. 25 March 1946.
12. 30 March 1946.
13. *Good Reading,* April 1964.

The unbristling beard:
Aristotle on poetry[*]

That's that, said God; and in emulation of Homer,
He nodded.

In the history of human discomfort, it would be hard to say whether it is Aristotle or St. Paul that has caused the greater sum total of sheer hell; but for the average undergraduate, the question is not a question. The Mesopotamian neuroses of the Bible are not often set

[*] No one, in 1967, can take up this wretched topic without intellectual gratitude to Gerald F. Else's *Aristotle's Poetics: The Argument* (Cambridge, Mass., 1957), but I should like to express esteem as well. This is one of those admirably complete books that any Classics scholar aspires to, but that few have the brains, the judgment, the staggering patience, and the sheer happy energy to produce. No one can possibly agree with Professor Else at every point. But who would wish to bore a man of Professor Else's ability with the mere echoing platitudes of agreement? 1

before him, but the *Poetics,* the *Rhetoric,* and the miserable *Ethics* are—and this, mind you, not in graduate school, when he is equipped to deal with nonsense and can transfer it, subdivided for oblivion, to small clean white cards, but as a mere child in college still sniffling with the self-pity that is his birthright. This is no state for exposure to Aristotle. It is a state when Answers is what we want; whether they are right or not is altogether secondary; and the attraction of Aristotle for a credulous humanity is that he *is* the man with the book of answers. And so the massive legend persists and is perpetuated, and, generation after college generation, the *Poetics* is foisted upon the innocent with as little intellectual misgiving as if it were of value to serious criticism, or even worth reading.

What therefore I shall try to do here is warn; and the warning will be directed, despite the steady sluicings of Greek, to the non-Classicist. It is he who is helpless; for it is he, poor devil, who has nothing between him and illusion but somebody else's translation and the off-chance that it is right. And it happens that Aristotle's language is in general so philosophically colorless that turning it into English involves not rendering but rewriting. For example 47a19 οἱ μὲν διὰ τέχνης οἱ δὲ διὰ συνηθείας, which Professor Else translates "some through art, some through habit and routine," I myself have always thought of as something like "both with and without formal training." Either is right; yet unless even a Classicist had the Greek text before him, and in many cases an *apparatus criticus* as well, it might never occur to him that Else and I were translating the same passage. But the ambition of every translator, though no one but a person of coarse feeling would say so, is to produce a page on which every sentence flows limpid and untroubled to its punctuable end, even if in the original it does not. And how is the non-Classicist to know?

Worse, there is at every point the question whether it was Aristotle or some Byzantine simpleton that wrote the words the page spreads before our exasperated eyes. Nobody who cannot read Greek can indeed have any real notion of the state the text of the *Poetics* is in. As a brief sample, do we at 55a33 read $<μᾶλλον>$ ἤ ("more than") or just ἤ ("or"), meaning respectively "poetry is an art for the sensitive $\left\{\begin{array}{l}\text{rather than}\\ \text{or}\end{array}\right\}$ the manic to practice"? *Rather than* certainly "makes more sense" in so far as the general point of the passage is that the poet must keep an unemotional eye on matters of detail (and as more Aristotelian-sounding anyhow). Yet Aristotle has also just been saying that a ranting scene calls for rant, and hence *perhaps* the association; moreover why should he have introduced the manic temperament at all unless as somehow comparable with the εὐφυής?

Perhaps the best way to give the non-Classicist an idea of what a mess the text makes is by quoting verbatim Else's working version of 49a15ff:

> Namely, on the one hand Aeschylus first raised the company of 'actors' from one to two and diminished the choral odes and gave the dialogue the leading role, [and Sophocles three (actors) and scene-painting] [furthermore the amplitude out of little stories and $<$sub-

limity of diction out of?> ludicrous diction; <for?>
thanks to its having grown out of satyr-play it was late
in acquiring seriousness] and on the other hand the
verse changed to iambic (trimeter) in place of (trochaic)
tetrameter.

Which parts of this are Aristotle's, which interpolation?
How much of it should we accept as fact no matter who
wrote it? It is hardly an exaggeration to say that here
no direction is up.

Yet even if a piece of text does not seem to be shreds
and patches, the precise meaning is likely to slither
through the fingers of Classicists and non-Classicists
alike. Let *mimesis* serve as a battered example. To Plato,
in the full vigor of approaching senility, a phrase like
μίμησίς τε καὶ ἀπεικασία (*Laws* 668b) is an angry indict-
ment, *mimesis* being a counterfeit presentment, not
Truth; but to Aristotle *mimesis* is simply a description,
scientific in intention, of what he thinks the creative intelligence is up to. The point that escaped him (and escapes his myriads of disciples still) is that an artist's
processes of "imitation" (portrayal) of something are not
really subject to this kind of objective equation. In a
passage at the start of Chapter 2, Aristotle is saying that
writers imitate

ἤτοι βελτίονας ἢ καθ' ἡμᾶς ἢ καὶ χείρονας ἢ καὶ τοιούτους ὥσπερ
οἱ γραφεῖς· Πολύγνωτος μὲν γὰρ κρείττους Παύσων δὲ χείρους
Διονύσιος δὲ ὁμοίους εἴκαζεν. (48a4)

"people either better than the generality (ἢ καθ' ἡμᾶς),
or worse, or simply like (ὁμοίους), just as painters do—

Polygnotus's portraits being nobler-looking than their subjects but Pauso's less noble, and Dionysius's simple unstylized likenesses." Or so it *might* be translated. But there is an ambiguity hidden in this which Aristotle seems not to have considered. Let me suppose the following description of the subject-matter of three of our most gifted woman writers:

> Mrs. Hutchins μιμεῖται women more sexual ἢ καθ' ἡμᾶς and Miss Porter less sexual and Miss Welty ὁμοίας.

This says that they are all portraying the same pretty thing but that each sees her (or anyhow portrays her) as something the others do not. On the other hand, if I write that

> People who sat for Franz Hals were pinker ἢ καθ' ἡμᾶς and Rembrandt's sitters less pink, and similarly El Greco's had long necks but Rubens's on the whole no necks at all,

what I am talking about is the relative pinkness and scrawniness of people rich enough to afford various first-rank portraitists, and this is quite another thing from the subjective opinions of three exquisitely subjective women about the μαχλοσύνη of their sex. A reader of the *Poetics* cannot ever be sure that Aristotle and his commentators have sorted this difference out.

To sum up, then, so far, for the non-Classicist:

I do not see how we can expect to be improved by the *Poetics* when we are constantly uncertain what Aristotle in fact wrote, and, even when we are certain, unable to agree on what he means.

But the non-Classicist should be told that he will encounter in the *Poetics* still a third ambiguity, whose
presence he is the less likely to suspect in that Aristotle
did not suspect it himself. It pained Aristotle to con-
template parts of the universe

> *that decline*
> *To stay where they belong, in line;*

and this sometimes led to his stretching his descriptive
terminology, thence to an imperceptible semantic drift,
and thence finally into a statement which overconfi-
dence in his term prevented his seeing was on the brink
of nonsense.

I offer as example the word οἰκεῖον. It means in the
Poetics "appropriate," "germane," "inherent in," and
the like; for instance, 48b24

> Historically, poetry-writing split along innate lines (κατὰ
> τὰ οἰκεῖα ἤθη); for the better classes used to portray noble
> life and conduct in odes and so on, and commoners or-
> dinary life—to begin with, in lampoons . . . Meters
> came along accordingly . . . some early poets writing
> in heroic meters, some in the iambics of lampoon.

The innateness is the poets' not the poetry's, and the
κατὰ τὴν οἰκείαν φύσιν of 49a4 confirms this. Yet right before our eyes what begins as simple quasi-historical
speculation on how different meters came about, ends
up as good as saying that meters have fixed inherent
characteristics and necessarily connote given themes.
And once the drift has occurred, it is absorbed and be-

comes standard procedure: the statement that "trial and error" (ἀπὸ τῆς πείρας 59b31) assigned hexameter to epic glides imperceptibly over into "the very nature of epic (αὐτὴ ἡ φύσις 60a4) teaches us to pick the right meter," and the same words αὐτὴ ἡ φύσις account for the introduction of iambics into tragedy—"its very nature found the proper meter" (49a24). Aristotle would be put to it to explain exactly which φύσις (out of half a dozen) taught the ancients to pick the elegiac distich or the French that chameleon the alexandrine, or for that matter Burns the Burns stanza and Housman the Housman. And what verse is οἰκεῖον, *Romeo and Juliet* or *Lear*?

This logical blind spot about prosody's having οἰκεῖα ἤθη or given characteristics is connected, psychologically at least, with the daunting sentence 49a13,

κατὰ μικρὸν ηὐξήθη προαγόντων ὅσον ἐγίγνετο φανερὸν αὐτῆς, καὶ πολλὰς μεταβολὰς μεταβαλοῦσα ἡ τραγῳδία ἐπαύσατο ἐπεὶ ἔσχε τὴν αὐτῆς φύσιν.

"Tragedy developed little by little as new possibilities in the form appeared, and after many changes over many years stopped when it attained its own nature." "Ἐπαύσατο"! Are we to understand that tragedy "paused" for Aristotle's convenience while he defined it, or that it stopped for good in obedience to his definition? This strange assumption that an art form must at some time or other necessarily reach perfection, and remain thereafter through eternity as ἱκανὸν τῷ αὐτοῦ εἴδει as Plato's most cosseted Idea, is as melancholy a perversion of τὸ οἰκεῖον as our own critics' who every decade, as the novel modulates a little, announce that the novel is dead. Art continues and forms continue, and Aristotle's own "little by little" should have reminded him how.

Perhaps only a disciple of Plato's would have fallen into this particular kind of aesthetic error, the fallacy of perfecting forms. Sophoclean tragedy, Ovidian elegiacs, the couplets of Pope—each type *looks as if* it had "stopped when it attained its own nature." But in what sense are these "perfections" of a given form rather than, quite simply, individual styles within a form? Are they more perfect, because later and so forth, than Aeschylean tragedy, Propertian elegiacs, and the couplets of Dryden? Or put another way, are Aristotle's great exemplars Homer and Sophocles *not* full of imperfections of form?

The groping non-Classicist, finally, is likely to be handicapped by awe: since he cannot read the Classics, they loom and take on giant size, charged with portent and uninterpretable grandeur. Yet there is of course nothing very special about τραγῳδία beyond its having a couple of first-rank playwrights. As Professor Else very justly says,[2] the connotation is just "a serious play"—upper-class life with upper-class problems, to be more explicit; and the non-Classicist should remind himself that most of our Indo-European literature is just such accounts of highly privileged people complaining with the utmost eloquence that (in George Price's phrase) a swarm of bees is out to get them, and how can such things be permitted to happen to privileged people anywhere. Priam said he had put up with more sheer outrage than any man in recorded history—

ἔτλην δ᾽ οἷ᾽ οὔ πώ τις ἐπιχθόνιος βροτὸς ἄλλος·

The sentiment is our most fertile literary platitude. One must in short see Greek literature for what it is, and not for instance be impressed by the Homeric hero's ἄσβεστον μένος when it is nothing but the bellowing Irish rage normal to the Indo-European male. Warn the purpling oaf that his tantrums'll be the end of him—φθίσει σε τὸ σὸν μένος—and what reply do you get? Οὐδέ με πείσεις: Nobody's telling *me* what to do! Οὐδ᾽ Ἕκτορα θυμὸν ἔπεισεν— Hector paid no attention to sensible advice either.

2

Probably the greatest single source of aesthetic mistake in the *Poetics* is its obsessive schema-making. In a realm where every creative experience indicates that Aristotelian order is not possible, order is exactly what Aristotle expected to find first, and so did find. This is why he can without a qualm compare tragedy and epic to determine which is "better": if there is order then necessarily there is an order of excellence. After all, οὐκ ἔοικεν ἡ φύσις ἐπεισοδιώδης οὖσα ὥσπερ μοχθηρὰ τραγῳδία (1090b19)—it hardly stands to reason that nature is as badly organized as a picaresque novel. If Heaven is sensible, its ways are ours. The predictable result, in the *Poetics,* is that the interminable classification is often too abstract to fit the actual literature it purports to classify, with no place for Archilochus or Aristophanes on the one hand yet on the other a prescription for the best sort of plot that fits only a handful of extant plays. Again, Aristotle's "*a priori* ideas shape his 'history' [of Greek literary genres] to the point of actual distortion." [3] Due moreover to the concealed assumptions, analysis of form imperceptibly adds further distortion by imposing or suggesting scales of value. Yet all we have at the end, after pages of philosophical gesticulation, is the deflating conclusion that the Tragic Flaw is just the ungrandiose and largely mechanical mistake of not recognizing your own relatives when you meet them.[4]

What is back of this sort of thing, psychologically speaking, is beyond doubt the defective aesthetic sensibility which Aristotle shares with the lightless armies of his disciples, all about us on every campus still. What moved Aristotle? Language, that moves us all? He did not think so.

δεῖ γὰρ . . . οὕτω συνεστάναι τὸν μῦθον ὥστε τὸν ἀκούοντα . . . καὶ φρίττειν καὶ ἐλεεῖν ἐκ τῶν συμβαινόντων. . . . ἐπεὶ δὲ τὴν ἀπὸ ἐλέου καὶ φόβου διὰ μιμήσεως δεῖ ἡδονὴν παρασκευάζειν τὸν ποιητήν, φανερὸν ὡς τοῦτο ἐν τοῖς πράγμασιν ἐμποιητέον. (53b3ff)

"The *plot* must be so constructed that you shudder with pity at how it works out. And since the playwright has to move his audience by portraying, obviously this emotion of theirs has to be built into the action." What moves you is peripety, in Sophocles as in O. Henry; in fact the only fair way to judge a play is *by* its plot (56a8). Language can accordingly have very little to do with it—

$$\text{ἅπαντα φαντασία ταῦτ' ἐστὶ καὶ πρὸς τὸν ἀκροάτην} \ldots (1404a11)$$

"all that part is imagination and for the listener." Aristotle did not see that it is not action as action that produces the illusion of action, but the handling of *language:* with Sir Herbert Read, he didn't "bother about the writing." As in that famous definition of tragedy in Chapter 6, style is just ἡδυσμένος λόγος, "sweetened" language: there is no organic unit of thing-said but (i) a thought which then (ii) is somehow "decorated" (as κοσμηθῆναι 49a29). *Le dessin et la couleur ne forment pas du tout un tout,* and it is Cézanne who is impenetrable.

It is possible to argue, from a passage in the *Rhetoric,* that Aristotle's apparent numbness was, instead, a bracketing of aesthetic perception with the learning instinct. At 1371b4 he says that it is a pleasure to μανθάνειν and θαυμάζειν painting, sculpture, and literature—"learn about" and "wonder at" being the meanings, but "wonder at" in what sense? Well, possibly a Boeotian gaping, jaw ajar; but also possibly it is Aristotle's attempt at describing aesthetic delight, and certainly his bursting out with such a word as "marvelous" about Homer (θεσπέσιος 59a30) suggests, even in a passage on structure, some form of genuine aesthetic experience. And yet if so, then why merge it (and lose its meaning) in μανθάνειν? And how explain that the *Poetics* hasn't a word on the choral lyric? I am not sure Else's sardonic phrase goes

far enough, that "Aristotle regarded the audible gar-
ment of poetry as, when all was said and done, an un-
fortunate necessity.[5] I suggest, as Else himself seemed
earlier to be implying,[6] that Aristotle did not really
grasp the way creative language operates.

This appears in his random remarks on writers. In
principle, Aristotle, like anyone else in his right mind,
recognized that the poet is an individual being with a
particular sort of endowment. As he says in Chapter 4,
everybody can imitate and has a sense of melody and
rhythm, but poets are "particularly gifted in these re-
spects," οἱ πεφυκότες πρὸς αὐτά (48b22); being so, they
"cause" art. Whether the "cause" of Picasso's *Guernica*
is the same as the "cause" when he is just playing with
art is an etiological investigation that I leave to a specialist—say, a medievalist seated in a labyrinth. But principle aside (a convenient place for it) Aristotle's history
of literature has an extraordinarily mechanized look.
Tragedy somehow seems to find its form, and appropriate meters to dictate their use, untouched by human
hand; and perhaps most sadly diagnostic of all is a passage in Chapter 4 that appears never to have caused
commentators a qualm:

οὐ περὶ πολλὰ γένη αἱ τραγῳδίαι εἰσίν· ζητοῦντες γὰρ οὐκ ἀπὸ
τέχνης ἀλλ᾿ ἀπὸ τύχης εὗρον τὸ τοιοῦτον παρασκευάζειν ἐν τοῖς
μύθοις. (54a9)

"tragic scenarios draw on a few families' [misfortunes,
for the mythology makes good material] as writers discovered, by chance not by art." But how, short of a
voice from Heaven, did they know *what* they had dis-

covered? If I am no more of an artist than to stumble upon my splendid effects by chance, then how on earth am I enough of an artist to know that effects are what they are, much less splendid ones? *Petitio principii* runs in fact through the whole structure of Aristotle's view of the artist. If everybody imitates and has melody and rhythm, why doesn't everyone, not just the artist, create? Πεφυκὼς πρὸς αὐτά is no more an answer than Plato's φύσει τινί in the *Apology:* if some people create more than other people because they are more creative, then, God help us, the reason must be that people who are less creative create less.

And as Aristotle had little real notion of what a writer is up to, his notions of the process of creation are wide of the mark too. Chapter 22 is typical: you start out with "the proper words" (τῶν κυρίων ὀνομάτων 58a19) which are really *saying* what you want to say, and only then fiddle around making them into fine language. The meaning is one thing; the λέξις, the "phrasing," another. This is how Ben Jonson told Drummond of Hawthornden he wrote and no doubt we must partly believe it, if only because *Finnegans Wake* was composed in somewhat the same way. But who under the sun else? The best I can do to help Aristotle's sense here is to suggest that he had somehow misunderstood the process of revision.[7]

Aristotle's personal difficulties with the arts also reappear in his contradictory attempts at defining aesthetic pleasure in the *Poetics.* In Chapter 14 the "appropriate pleasure" is an emotion produced by a *mimesis,* but in Chapter 23 it comes not from imitation at all but from a kind of structural proportion in the plot. This latter is the familiar Greek trope: arrangement, symmetry, and proper demarcation are called "the main aspects of the beautiful" in the *Metaphysics* (1078a36). But the insistent repetition of the *mimesis* concept throughout the *Poetics,* even unexplained, would make that seem far the likelier meaning for Aristotle to have had in mind if it were not for one sentence in Chapter 4. He has just been saying that one enjoys a work of art because one recognizes the object it imitates; but then "if one happens *not* to have seen [the imitated object] before, the pleasure will not be in its being a likeness but in the artist's skill or the finish or for some similar reason." Then, "learning something" and "delighting in the contemplation of copies" are not necessarily why art appeals to us after all: there are other reasons, and less badly stated ones. What *mimesis* means in Aristotle may be behavior natural to children and Macedonians, but hardly to artists. In any case, when he comes to explaining "what we mean by saying 'artistically' " (τὸ δὲ καλῶς τί λέγομεν 53b26) I fail to see how all this spiritual window-shopping is to apply anyhow, for what he in fact calls finest are the most revolting situations that mythological ingenuity could devise—matricide, fratricide, incest, cannibalism, infanticide, and the constupration of one's handiest female relatives.

I suggest that the trouble comes from a conflation of two sorts of definition—(i) a statement about literature: Aristotle's calling tragedy "a portrayal of life and action" (μίμησις πράξεως καὶ βίου 50a16) is of the order of our modern remark that a character or a book is "alive";

and (ii) a statement about human behavior: *mimesis*, more or less automatically, moves us. The conflation has veiled the logical flaws. How for example would Aristotle account for the case of one spectator's being moved but another's not? How, again, explain that Crusoe's Friday seems real enough to me though I have never seen a cannibal, or that, though innocent of incest, I can be certain that nearly all literary treatments of the theme are superficial to the point of aberration? [8] Generally speaking, we today make (i) the basis of our assessments; Aristotle, with his eye on (ii), forgot to what extent assessment has to be accounted for.

In practice Aristotle's own likes and dislikes shaped his theory; but such mere consequences of human vanity are inadmissible, metaphysically speaking, so the process is presented the other way round. Plot is the big thing (τὸ μέγιστον 50a15), so logically enough Aeschylus is barely mentioned; but Homer is θεσπέσιος, so more plot-construction is discovered in Homer than the Homeridae would ever have been likely to lay claim to. And over and over, *one* type of tragedy—the bloodiest—comes close to being held up to us as universal Rule.

3

But one of the paradoxes of the *Poetics* is that while unless you can read Greek you can't make sense of more than half of it, yet if you can read Greek this is just the half you despair of making sense of; and the aesthetic ricochet I have been deploring is, unhappily, not its only form of intellectual mishap. What might be called, if one's nerves could stand it, the intussusception of literature by philosophy is a depressing process, even with modern asepsis and nicety of tolerances; in the *Poetics,* back at the gaudy start of it all, there is, in a phrase of Miss Compton-Burnett's,[9] "a freedom from any kind of subtlety" that should make even a disciple think twice. This takes several forms, of which the easiest to dissect out and define is irrelevance.

My own favorite is the *arché-méson-teleuté* nonsense. Nobody has ever said how a play could *not* have a beginning, a middle, and (in due course) an end; but Aristotle, like General Eisenhower, found a deep satisfaction in the enucleation of the obvious, and so we get 50b27ff:

> A 'beginning' is what doesn't have to come after something else but that something else exists *to* come after; and conversely an 'end' is something that either has to be, or generally is, after something else, with nothing else after it; and a 'middle,' what is itself after something and has after it something else. So, well-made plots must not begin just anywhere and end just anywhere, but do as prescribed.

But the trouble with this sort of *recitativo* is not so much that it is pointless as that its lack of point can lead to confusion. I will instance the famous anatomy of tragedy: a play is constituted of these, and only these, six "parts"—*mythos* (structure or plot), τὰ ἤθη (the characters' characteristics), *dianoia* (thought), *lexis* (speech), *melopoeia* (the choral side), and *opsis* (the visual side).[10]

This sounds wonderfully definitive; we are moreover told it is. Yet not only is there nothing one can *do* with such a description critically (as Aristotle himself found out) but it could hardly be more arbitrary, and is not exhaustive. There is for example only one category for the eye, as against several for the ear and the mind (from an actor's or director's standpoint either *lexis-melopoeia-opsis* make one homogeneous category or *opsis* wants subdividing into costume, stage-machinery, etc.). Worse, there is the tedious confusion of lumping together, as if they were six things of a kind, what look like three entirely disparate levels of category: (1) production (*opsis*), (2) the writing (*mythos-lexis-melopoeia*), and (3) the misty abstracts, "spiritual make-up" (τὰ ἤθη) and "thought." This confusion moreover Aristotle immediately makes worse still by putting the perfectly concrete *mythos* in the abstract group and then sorting out the six "parts" into three groups from a different standpoint altogether: (1) *lexis* and *melopoeia* are "what they imitate by means of," (2) *opsis* is the "how," and (3) *mythos*-temperament-thought, the "what."

Since "they" here means the actors, the intellectually respectable way to straighten the muddle out ought to be to make τὰ ἤθη and *dianoia* concrete too; and this, it turns out, can be done by seeing how Aristotle uses these terms elsewhere when he is doing something practical with them.

τὰ δὲ ἤθη καθ᾽ ἃ ποιούς τινας εἶναί φαμεν τοὺς πράττοντας
διάνοια δὲ ἐν ὅσοις λέγοντες ἀποδεικνύασί τι ἢ καὶ ἀποφαίνονται
γνώμην. (50a5)

"We say 'character' meaning a person is such-and-such judging by what he does, and 'thought' meaning when he conveys information or ideas."

τὸ λέγειν δύνασθαι τὰ ἐνόντα καὶ τὰ ἁρμόττοντα. . . . ἔστι δὲ ἦθος μὲν . . . ὃ δῆλοι τὴν προαίρεσιν. . . . διάνοια δὲ ἐν οἷς ἀποδεικνύασί τι ὡς ἔστιν ἢ ὡς οὐκ ἔστιν ἢ καθόλου τι ἀποφαίνονται·

Thought means "being able to say something that fits the situation; 'character,' what explains the character's choices. . . . Thought [is speeches] in which they argue that something is or isn't so, or dramatic exposition generally." [11] Now, we know nothing of fourth-century tragedy and hence may well be missing whatever point Aristotle thought he was making; but what he *says* is indisputable: τὰ ἤθη denotes dialogue that furthers the action, the dramatic development of character and plot, and *dianoia* denotes non-dramatic dialogue, such as spot eloquence or as exposition, and apparently also (in Chapter 19) speeches designed to rouse audience emotion. All of which is as concrete as one can ask for.

But then why are these two kinds of speeches not subdivisions of *lexis,* speech itself? and so back we go into the immemorial pastime of setting still another Aristotelian term to endlessly chasing its tail: what is *lexis*?

Well, at 49a23 it is just trimeters as opposed to tetrameters; but 49b34 looks temporarily more helpful: "I define *lexis* as the actual composition of verse." But then comes 50b13: "I define *lexis,* as said before, as the expressing of thought in language"—which is not what he said before at all. One definition adds up to prosody, the other to *dianoia.* And there is still a third shot at it in the *Rhetoric:*

οἱ γὰρ γραφόμενοι λόγοι μεῖζον ἰσχύουσι διὰ τὴν λέξιν ἢ διὰ τὴν διάνοιαν,[12]

which I cite in the loyal Aristotelian certainty that it will confuse us all further still, for it seems to mean that writing gets its effects by how it is written rather than by what it says. But my point is that it keeps *dianoia* and *lexis,* as in the six "parts," *separate* terms; and how does even a philosopher manage legerdemain like that? Translating *lexis* "diction" can't be made to fit either; and in a word we are left with the esoteric choice between saying either that there are two sorts of speech in tragedy, neither of which is speech, or that the composition of dialogue for drama does not result in dramatic dialogue. I am half inclined to take the Psalmist's word for it—*There is neither speech nor language; lo, without these their voice is heard.*[13]

It must in fairness be kept in mind that a share of the impenetrabilities of the *Poetics* is due not to Aristotle's lapses but to our own. We for example do not see what is right there before our eyes: Aeschylus's plays have exhibited their three actors to our attention for some twenty-four centuries, yet until Else pointed this out to us a decade or so ago we stoutly maintained that three actors didn't come in until Sophocles, and that Aristotle was no more able to count up to three than we were. Or again, and alas more generally, to make sense for ourselves of what Aristotle's text actually says, we first assume that he must mean something that makes sense specifically to *us;* and having assumed the meaning a passage ought to have we then proceed to the natural business of finding that meaning in the passage.

Yet the fact of inconsistency remains, in section after section. Some may no doubt be extenuated as later insertions after an unnoticed change of emphasis or even of mind, as, for example, the disagreement between Chapters 2 and 15 about how dramatists should portray nobility of character, or the fact that the *desis* and *lysis* of Chapter 18 ought to, but do not, appear in Chapter 7. But change of emphasis will not exonerate the larger inconsistencies. Aristotle's (and the natural) view of tragic action is that "the artistic plot necessarily has its shift of circumstance from a happy estate to adversity or ruin" (53a13); yet in the very next chapter, when he comes to ranking the various modes of tragic scenario, he lays it down that the best or "strongest" (κράτιστον) ending is the type in which X is about to kill Y, not knowing (*hamartia*) that Y is a relative, but (*anagnórisis*) recognizes him just in time. The contradiction is inscrutable. There are, again, the multiple inconsistencies about the epic—it must have its own laws yet ought to follow the practice of tragedy; it ought to follow the practice of tragedy but pity and fear are left out; its length and variety of incident are one of its advantages in Chapter 24 but in Chapter 26 one of its drawbacks.

There is, finally, a specialized form of exasperation to which the non-Classicist is immune, the interminable clumsiness of Aristotle's language—passage after passage in which, though what he says presumably makes sense, the way he says it confounds the reason. A simple instance is his prescription in Chapter 17 for handling plot-outline. Whether your scenario is traditional or original, he says, you must start by disregarding whoever your characters may be, names and all, and lay out the story καθόλου (whatever this means here, generally it means "generally"): and only then, when your plot is worked out, are you to detail your episodes ὑποθέντα τὰ ὀνόματα, dubbing in your characters' names. The mind reels: we are to plan a story about a traveler who kills an old man in a crossroads brawl without knowing it is his father and who then marries a widowed queen without knowing she is his mother, but we are not to let it cross our minds that we may, eventually, assign this character the name Oedipus.

One's first thought is to take refuge from this nonsense in the καθόλου of 51b8, meaning in this case "universal":

the universal . . . is what writing aims at, assigning names as a secondary and subsequent matter (ἐπιτιθεμένη),

which I take to be Aristotle's way of saying that the point about character is not that your characters have specific names but that they be alive or believable or some such workable adjective. This is how comedy-writers lay out plots, he adds a few lines later; and for all we know he had in mind something in the plays of his contemporaries; no fourth-century tragedy survives to prove the thing one way or the other. I tend to conclude, as Professor Else seems to do,[14] that what Aristotle was trying to say is that the traditional story comes encrusted with episodes, that they tend to be random and heterogeneous, and that the writer must pick out just those that are "thematic" (as we might today translate ἁρμόττοντα) and appropriate to his handling of the story. But why then not say so in so many words? Is the precept so noticeably distant from platitude that it could not have been stated in primer Greek?

4

If Professor Else's description of the *Poetics* is recited in tones of suitable deprecation, it is a fair description enough: "not a discussion of 'poetry' in . . . any sense of the English term; [but] in all sadness and sobriety, an analysis of the nature and functioning of the *art* of poetry and of [two of] its species." [15] On the epic, it is nearly zero; but on tragedy it does make a number of points that, for certain types of play, are mildly practical, for example one must not only see that one's characters and episodes are not random but must put them together preserving a look of logical or necessary sequence (δι ἄλληλα). There are structural hints of one kind and another: your audience gets the biggest dramatic shock when pity and terror come about unexpectedly, though still logically, and so on. The famous ὅρος τοῦ μήκους—the norm of length that caused pitched battles long ago when it was one of the Classical Unities —has at least an historical interest, and Else even finds it "the most important strictly aesthetic principle in the *Poetics,* and the one to which Aristotle devotes the most attention." [16] The purely mechanical side of the analysis is moreover often acute: for instance, the well-made interaction of situation, character, and peripety that will produce the most hair-raising *coups de théâtre* is set out in detail. Aristotle, unlike Plato, was at least *looking* at literature.

But he was badly equipped to describe what he saw. What the eager Ph.D. mind can read into the *Poetics* is one thing; what the *Poetics* in fact *says* is another, and an even duller. It is really useful only to those who are not concerned with literature anyhow—a mine where Aristotelian scholars can pursue their sunless labors, the slag at the pit-head a *scavo* for aesthetic archaeology. It can, again, serve professors of less showy literatures for the display of elegant misquotation. But of what earthly use to the critic or the writer is a dissection of literature by a marine biologist? He does have the virtue, as against Plato, of not expecting poetry to impart nonexistent metaphysical truths: he sees that the business of a work of art is exactly what Plato condemned it for, that it moves one. But the *Poetics* is none the less a breviary on how to write by a man who did not understand writing. It opens with sweep and grandeur, and one murmurs in a kind of awe ὡς σεμνὸς ὁ κατάρατος; yet all it amounts to is the formulae of a how-to; and all the subsequent centuries of dialectical ingenuity have not succeeded in demonstrating that the majestic exordium illumines or is even necessarily related to the hodge-podge the treatise ends in. Its intellectual limits are thoroughly, though I think unwittingly, fixed by a sentence of Professor Else's: "The ultimate root of the tragic is ignorance, and its actualization is the conversion of ignorance into knowledge, but with the proviso that the ignorance must have led or threatened to lead to an act which runs counter to man's deepest moral instincts." [17] Well, said Pindar, σοφὸς ὁ πολλὰ ϝειδὼς φυᾷ —which as good as means the artist is born knowing better.[18]

For, finally, what does this *Art of Poetic Composition* tell a student about composition or about poetry? The answer is: nothing. What does it tell about the very way a play *becomes* a play, the writing? Nothing. Nor does it help—it hardly crossed Aristotle's mind that it's important—to perform the aesthetic assessments that must come before everything else. The *Poetics* cannot even help me decide whether

> ὦ δεῦρ᾽ ὁδοιποροῦντος εὐβύρσοις ποσί
> ξένου κάρηνον

is the ingenious translation, or the mighty original, of Housman's

> *O suitably attired in leather boots*
> *Head of a traveler . . .*

Whom, for that matter, can we even suppose the *Poetics* was written for? The creative intelligence knew it all already, and more; in Pindar's phrase, the creative intelligence is born with it. *"Ces passages enharmoniques, dont le cher oncle a fait tant de train,"* said Rameau's nephew to Diderot, *"ce n'est pas la mer à boire, nous nous en tirons."*

NOTES

1. A sample dissent: At 49b10 μεγάλη μίμησις strikes me as being no more convincing Greek than his translation of it, "large-sized imitation," is English. I should argue that a form of μέγα is unlikely here: (i) size throughout the *Poetics*, e.g. 49b25, is equated with μῆκος (as against μικροὶ λόγοι, etc.), and here μήκει is the key word in the *following* sentence; (ii) μετὰ λόγου looks like a gloss, and if so, then what it displaced was by all odds some set of letters that did *not* resemble it.

   Nor in this same passage can I follow the argument that "tragedy tries to be, exist, in a certain space of time" (p. 210) instead of the perfectly straightforward "day" of the Classical Unities. The median length of Sophoclean-Euripidean tragedy is a mere 1450 lines: there can hardly be a question of occupying a chronology in Else's sense. What then remains but dramatic time?—with μικρὸν ἐξαλλάττειν meaning "vary a little plus or minus." I see no greater logic in Else's "minus" than in other people's "plus." See also Note 16 below.

2. Else, p. 330, note.

3. *Ibid.*, p. 145.

4. The principles "were based too narrowly to begin with": Else, p. 446. Professor Else is too kind. If *I* observed that my offspring resembled a centaur, I should recalculate the odds against my wife's (or my) being—whether I had noticed it before or not—a horse.

5. Else, p. 235.

6. *Ibid.*, p. 52.

7. Another odd blunder is 50a35: beginners are better at phrasing and character-drawing than at plot-construction. The very opposite is true.

8. I except the pervasive incest and in-law adultery in Miss Compton-Burnett's novels, where however the theme has a largely choral character, with no *approfondissement* intended.

9. *A House and Its Head* (London, 1935), Chap. 2.

10. Also called ὁ τῆς ὄψεως κόσμος (49b32), "the orderly handling of visual effect." Both expressions are variously understood: mere costuming, mere stage effects, the whole visual side of production, and so on.

11. As Else says (p. 245), "the delimitation of the two terms gave Aristotle trouble." I find among old notes a dry suggestion of Sutherland's: "Thought is what goes on in dialogue."

12. III, i, 7. What is said about *lexis* in Chapter 19 of the *Poetics* seems to me too confused to comment on profitably.

13. *Psalms* 19, 3. The general confusion about the "parts" is compounded in Chapter 18:

   τραγῳδίας δὲ εἴδη εἰσὶ τέσσαρα, τοσαῦτα γὰρ τὰ μέρη ἐλέχθη (55b32): "there are four types of tragedy, for the parts were said to be four." This latter clause makes so little sense that Professor Else (p. 533) calls it "the remark of a well-meaning but inept reader," and Susemihl athetized it. Yet a few lines below we read γεγονότων . . . καθ᾽ ἕκαστον μέρος ἀγαθῶν ποιητῶν, "there have been poets good at each part," not "each kind." And just to top everything off, the "parts" that Aristotle actually does base aesthetic assessment on are neither these inexplicable four nor the original six they are here said to be, but another set of six altogether: peripety, recognition, size, pity-fear, *hamartía*, and *cátharsis*.

14. Else, p. 506.
15. *Ibid.*, p. 4.
16. *Ibid.*, p. 289. *The* point about μῆκος in Greek tragedy, however, strikes me as being that time is stylized, incidents happening not by sun time but as the action requires; and this, Aristotle says nothing about.
17. *Ibid.*, p. 420.
18. *Ol.* 2, 154.

Cornbread and circuses

"It must be a step of a kind, to be one of the family," said Miss Burtenshaw, "though not in any especial direction."

—I. Compton-Burnett,
A House and Its Head

The parochial nature of this essay owes much to the parochial nature of the festivities it reports on. I have however left it largely as first published: I could hardly hope for a blander illustration of the inanities, the insulsitas, *which this book was written to reprehend. Princeton University stages an annual public-relations open house on its campus for near-by alumni and their wives, the feature being a mock-intellectual display by various groups of departments in turn: real professors hold real discussions on their subjects in real classrooms, and alumni and wives sign up for these and attend (and discuss) as if undergraduates still. What follows describes the performance in 1964.*

Alumni Day, with the shows and tea-fights our alma mater puts on then for those of us—undisabused, homesick, or merely over-tribal—who attend, is the one occasion in the year when an alumnus can totter in and sit down in wheezy judgment on the kind of thing his University is currently purveying. The University's own handouts naturally put it a little better: the product on display is "contributions made in [given] areas by Princetonians in relation to similar work by other contemporary Americans";[1] but in fact all that happens is that we shamble into a precept-room as if the world were still young, a faculty member does his customary stuff, and there is thus presented for our sentimental assessment a more or less honest sample of Princeton education as our sons and grandsons get it in 1964.

This time round, the precepts happened to be in architecture, drama, music, painting, and poetry—an ideal opportunity to judge how well or less well the traditions of Western culture are being handed down in a University whose president at least—$\theta a\hat{v}\mu a$ $i\delta\acute{\epsilon}\sigma\theta a\iota$—can read the language they began in.

I picked the precept in literature. There was a "recommended reading" that sounded both instructive and readable. A special issue of our *Library Chronicle* had been got out, entitled *Seven Princeton Poets:* a controlling 51 per cent of its page-space was filled with essays on the seven by members of the English faculty, and another 39 per cent with Library bibliography; and in effect therefore the Princeton English Department had hired a hall at a 39 per cent rental and was praying alumni attendance at a performance of its own prose.

I remembered an ambiguous anecdote of Xenophon's: Socrates and some companions had been passing an idle and enjoyable hour watching the lovely Theodote pose for a painter, and at the end Socrates said, "Should we thank Theodote for letting us look at her, or she us for looking?" But I loyally decided to risk the ambiguity. I am after all a responsible alumnus, one of that group whose cries of black and obscurantist rage fill the Letters column of the *Princeton Alumni Weekly* year after year; and I wanted to see for myself what was what.

I went also, perhaps I should say, representatively, in the spirit of the lines of the late Thomas Riggs '37:

> *Some saw blondes. I admit there are*
> *Such fabulous creatures and the unicorn,*
> *And that they lead poor poets many a dance.*

I went into the precept room, then, with only one presupposition, that a department of any literature ought to concern itself with what literature by and large *is,* what is trash and what is good in the canon and why, the importance universally of style and the triviality of most content. I presumed the pedagogical aim was to develop in undergraduates enough critical sense so that the unlettered alumnus will later be able, as he staggers blearily from weekend to weekend, to tell for himself which way, culturally speaking, is up. Art departments seem to accomplish this. In my time the Princeton English Department conspicuously did not. The question was, then, what about today?

This question, as it turned out, the precept failed to answer. There was a change in plan: two of the seven poets dropped in, Bink Noll '47 and Galway Kinnell '48, and the discussion that was to have been about them was with them. Yet this, as it happened, posed the question in a different form: why does the average Princeton graduate leave college with his concept of literature unchanged from what was foisted upon him in grammar school? For the precept discussion consisted almost wholly of questions by alumni and their wives as to what this or that poem of Noll's or Kinnell's "meant," what was its place in their "thought." Hardly one mention of good or bad lines, or of the nature of words, or of prosody; the simple noun "style" never occurred, nor did "lyric," though almost any poet is first of all a lyric poet; in short not a word to suggest that either man was anything but a *vates,* the fellow with the book of answers. The precept thus became simply Noll and Kinnell answering, with the most perfect courtesy, question after question whose unconscious implication was that the pair of them were not so much gifted writers as ungifted theologians.

Maxima debetur (in Dr. Spock's phrase) *puero reverentia;* and if years after graduation a B.A. persists in the grammar-school notion that literature is just a collection of decorated declarative sentences, we owe it to him to inquire why. Are English departments contributing to cultural delinquency? If they are, *how* are they doing it? I could have told how, in my own day, though English was not my department; but times change, times change; so I went home and read the professorial essays in *Seven Princeton Poets* to see what was new, or whether there was anything.

In part, there was not. If Dean Gauss's shade will forgive my adding a negative to a phrase he once leveled and discharged at me, I have never listened to such a fusillade of un-epigrams. *In a profound sense. Impact. Within the context of other themes. Deepened the exploration of his chosen subject-matter.* This was just how they used to talk about Wordsworth (though in the case of Wordsworth what difference does it make what you say); and along with this earnest diction there went, sure enough, as of old, the same well-remembered profusion of mispronouncement on concrete detail.

In the first of the essays, on Louis Coxe '40, the professorial commentary tells me that the poem "Marsh Hawk" illustrates the poet's "mastery over meter, rhyme, and stanzaic form, as well as his extraordinary economy of means." Most of us would take it for granted, rather than announce in the accents of discovery and surprise, that a poet had mastered the mere framework elements of his art by age thirty-five; but let us concede the commentator his innocence and look at the lines he gives the impression of describing. The poem begins

> *Before dew falls and dark has clutched horizon*
> *He comes, tilting with shadow from his marsh,*
> *Cruising the meadow, stooping and all vision*
> *For white-footed mice ascuttle under slash*

—and what at once appears is as good as the contrary of what was just said about meter, rhyme, stanza, and economy.

Whether Coxe is a master of meter I do not know; but *here* he is simply distorting meter to disguise the stanza he has found himself stuck with. For whether professorial circles know it or not, this particular quatrain is as unpromising a form as can be found in English. An unnerving specimen from the *Oxford Book of Victorian Verse* is Miss Brontë's

> *Today I will not seek the shadowy region;*
> *Its unsustaining vastness waxes drear;*
> *And visions rising, legion after legion,*
> *Bring the unreal world too strangely near.*

"Drear" is no word for it; it is hard to see how even a meat-loaf sensibility like Quiller-Couch's found it bearable. Coxe, like any man of talent, quite properly dissembles his predicament by prosodic means, drastic variations of meter, including an immediate four-beat line in the next stanza. Yet for all I can tell, we should be told in the lecture-hall that those showers of trochaic and anapestic substitution suggest the swoops of the hawk.

As to rhyme, the stanza above has none, nor have lines 1 and 3 in the other three stanzas; Mr. Coxe's critic must therefore regard *flight-night, cruel-jewel,* and *blood-flood* as "masterly." Well, we do not, like the French, delight in surprising ourselves with things like

> *L'univers se*
> *Bouleverse.*

But we do have standards: *swans-bronze* is good, *flood-blood* is boring. As Coxe of course knew; but here, rhyme didn't concern him.

As to that "extraordinary economy of means," which the commentary paraphrases as "a spare and chiseled style which dispenses with all gratuitous embellishment,"—well, so help me, a typical line is

He homes in on the fear that sweats the weather,

and in fact the language throughout is gaudy, intricate, headstrong, asyntactic, and overpowering. When therefore a critic calls it "reticent, slightly austere," the fair-minded conclusion may be that he had somehow mixed up his notes and was writing about another poem—even another poet—altogether.

Discussion of something that isn't really there is one way of leaving the undergraduate in his primal fog; they did it in my day too; but the comment on Kinnell displays something new. And if the one colleague hasn't seen what was before his eyes, the other might be said to have stared right through it and seen something still finer on the other side—himself, clothed in a radiance of language. The language is however not the standard English the Department professes, but a kind of dream-speak in which one talks of a poet's "commitment" and a poem's "strategy"; moreover, like this professor's own glossy phrase "nature as norm and enigma, the locus of revelation," it need not imply any real desire to communicate. But suppose it does. Here is his exposition of how Kinnell composes:

> Now if a poem re-enacts a moment of enlightenment in the poet's life, then it is a recreation; it is mimetic. But if the meaning is only dimly perceived beforehand and

the "unifying light" evolves in the creative act, then the poem itself becomes the moment of enlightenment: it is visionary.* . . . In the attempt to create a moment of enlightenment, its meaning may change and grow, so that the finished poem becomes the fulfillment of the moment of experience . . . the tension between these impulses [vision and *mimesis*] and their constantly shifting relationship seem to affect the form and style of individual poems, the lines of Kinnell's development, even his deepest intuitions of meaning.

A sentence-by-sentence English version of this, for the behoof of undergraduates, might run: "What a poet writes is stuff that comes into his head. Sometimes what he writes makes sense. Sometimes, though, he has to do a good deal of fiddling before it comes out in a particular way. Kinnell seems to have fiddled with some of his poems more than with others."

This is dull, I admit, compared to the original; it hardly seems as if one had to be a professor of English literature to think it up. Yet even the damage done here by translation could be useful in educating the grammar-school undergraduate mind: for it shows with a dreadful clarity that what is important, in imitation literature as in real, is not the content but the style. Translation is no more unkind to this particular piece of departmental English than it is to, say, Pindar, as magnificent a dull-content poet as Milton himself.

* His ear for the dialect is slightly at fault here: instead of "visionary" a birthright speaker would use the natural and colloquial "autanagnoristic."

Whence came this fashion, or a style so dense
With ev'ry known embellishment, save sense?

We all know that criticism became "difficult" in imitation of poetry, which Eliot (rather a long time ago now) said had to be "difficult" or it wouldn't explain what a terrible time he kept having. Today, in Berryman's sardonic phrase, even "some very able modern critics sound like computers, or wasps, or mediums." [2] The real question is, why does this sort of thing *persist?* The novelty should have worn off; surely only a kind of status-symbol status remains. What really wants explanation is why it is still considered criticism to do one's best to obfuscate what one is ostensibly doing one's best to shed light upon.

It persists, this book should have made clear, particularly in universities, for two reasons: ignorance of the creative process, and a portentous and interminable preoccupation with Meaning.

Most people who write about writers seem to know really very little about how writers write. As Malraux remarked in *Les Voix du Silence,*

> *Le non-artiste suppose que l'artiste procède comme il procéderait, lui, s'il faisait une oeuvre d'art, mais dispose de moyens plus puissants. Or le non-artiste ne "procéderait" pas du tout, car ce qu'il fait est souvenir, signe, récit, jamais oeuvre d'art.*[3]

The artist does something wholly different in kind: he creates. And often he creates blindly. Matisse wrote to Simon Bussy,

Je travaille sans théorie. J'ai seulement conscience des forces que j'emploie, et je suis poussé par mon idée que je ne connais vraiment qu'au fur et à mesure qu'elle se développe par la marche du tableau.[4]

Listen to Moravia's unwitting paraphrase:

> In writing a novel, there is in the beginning what I call a theme. It's not an idea but a feeling. Then this feeling goes on developing and unravelling itself, like a rope. That is why I say that a novel writes itself. One writes a novel in order to know why one writes it.[5]

All this the writer knows, and understands as automatically as a poet understands Malraux's

> *Le poète est obsédé par une voix à quoi doivent s'accorder les mots,*[6]

even though he doesn't know what this "voice" is, or whether it comes from his head or from the muscles of his throat and tongue.

But the average professor unhappily thinks he *can* tell you. For, surely, writing is a ratiocinative process! Why use words *unless* to mean something? He would not be so unsophisticated as to descry Meaning in, say, a concerto, nor does he share the proletarian conviction that what a painter is trying to paint into a picture is photographic likeness. Yet he cannot help talking as if he thought meaning were something one inescapably writes into a sentence. The born writer is unlikely to make this mistake: he is much too aware of style and of the incantatory and merely apolaustic uses of language to pay all that attention to meaning. Moreover he knows that words have tones and clefs and are of various tempos, or again can often be put onto paper as pigment is put onto a canvas. In fact any writer who is a mere meaning-writer is likely to be a non-artist in Malraux's sense (C. P. Snow is a grisly example), and what he writes is seldom literature. People think it is only because it corresponds to their own non-artist notion of how art is made.

If professors share this delusion, this is of course in part because of the nature of their job. For to be intelligible about style is admittedly not easy in the classroom. One's audience, for one thing, is *le bas peuple,* undergraduates. Nothing on the other hand is easier than hashing out a lecture or a *revue* piece on Meaning and Insights, or again on Movements and Wordsworth's theoretical natterings and why Gautier's *gilet* was green. There is also much more wordage in this kind of thing than in style. So literature is distorted and misdescribed by the literature describing it.

The most obvious distortion is the lack of balance the meaning-monger induces: he extols the gnomic (usually the pseudo-gnomic into the bargain) and slights everything else. In the nature of things this also involves paying far more attention to poetry than to novels, for since a poem is highly condensed, the time saved in reading it can be employed in writing about it at length. Moreover poetry is often so ambiguous that one can write almost anything about it without feeling intellectually nervous. But the drawback is that if one is dealing in Meanings one has to sound weighty or the thing doesn't come off. In consequence every poet has to be blown up into a major poet as far as commentary on him goes; and sure enough, right before our eyes a highly talented minor poet like Kinnell is worked over as if he were Auden. Or Dante.

Again, undergraduates are given to understand that writers write in accordance with formulated theories. The fact is that a writer writes as comes naturally (how else?) and then sometimes mocks up a manifesto afterwards as justification or—especially if French—as an extra piece of literature (or even just for the hell of it). Most writers of the first rank could echo Matisse's *Je travaille sans théorie;* even when they don't, their announced theories are as often as not irrelevant. Guillaume Apollinaire and Henry James were indefatigable theorists, yet where in Apollinaire is the brilliance of *Alcools* "explained," or where in the endless anaphora of James's prefaces can one learn what went wrong with *The Bostonians* or what "principle" made *The Golden Bowl* a Jamesian masterpiece? The emperor is as regrettably naked as ever, yet when my fellow alumni go out from our over-endowed alma mater they can furnish you with memorized descriptions of his clothes.

The greatest distortion, perhaps, is that if one is eager only to witch around for Meaning, one is likely to forget entirely the—normally preliminary and fundamental—question whether the piece of writing one is at work on is in fact worth working on at all. A bad page of Wordsworth makes just as much sense as a good one, and hence when one's eye is on the meaning everything tends to look the same. A practiced professor of English literature will thus often be honestly unable to tell when Wordsworth is writing trash, even though that is most of the time. So any critical faculty atrophies even in those who have such a thing.

Last of all, there is not even a practical or tool-box purpose in the manipulation of meaning: it cannot help you discriminate any better than it helped Wordsworth. As an *ad hominem* demonstration, pick any mature poem from *Seven Princeton Poets,* for example Bink Noll's charged and brilliant "Air Tunnel, Monticello," and balance against it semantically the following "Serpentine," by Alexander B. Griswold '28, from the *Nassau Literary Magazine* of December 1925.* I last saw Griswold fox-hunting his way through some Cantab. college or other a third of a century ago, and for all I know he had given up poetry even then; but here he is *aetat.* 19:

> *In sandarac etui for sepulchre*
>   *lies the cered body of a poisoned queen;*
>   *and in her mouth and hair, and at her feet,*
>   *and in the grey folds of her winding-sheet,*
>   *there sifts a dreamy powder, smooth and green,*
> *the magic of an idle sorcerer,*
>   *an ancient spell, cast when the shroud was spun.*
>   *In death her hands clutch amorously a bowl*
>   *that still contains the fragments of her soul,*
>   *a tale of Beauty sought, and Beauty won,*
> *his false lips kissed, and Beauty dead for her.*

---

* In a story in the same issue, by the way, Archer Winsten '26 had a derisive sentence which Dean Root's department of that untroubled day might well have meditated on: "If I ever saw an ugly, sincere, big-nosed, simple-looking ass, it's Wordsworth."

Now, the prosody of lines 5 and 6 might be bettered—
"dreamy" perhaps replaced by a dactyl but in any case
its *e*-sounds eliminated, and the next line recast entirely,
for it not only moves too fast but is flat (it is not just
chance how routine and lustreless the imagery becomes
exactly where the verse-movement goes wrong). But in
general Griswold's handling of sound, of pause, of the
sheer nonsense of the thing, is virtuoso work: it must
have been a pleasure to write. Phrasing like Noll's

> *The orifice smoking in the county of hope*

is of course way beyond Griswold's. But does *meaning*
tell you it is? Or tell you anything whatever about either
poem as poem? What are they "about"? I see no way of
demonstrating that what English departments call the
"immediacy" of either is less or greater than the other's.
The two *fashions* of meaning of course differ as much
as the topics and the styles.

If then Meaning is pedagogically useless, what can one
dole out to the undergraduate instead? I suggest a re-
turn to what Europe has never abandoned, despite
Sartre and Camus—the close attention to style and to
literary form. This means, in poetry, far more concern
for the lyric element: after all, if *this* falls below a vary-
ing but understood percentage, we tend to agree in defining the result as something other than "poem."

To show what I mean in its simplest form, here, in
peroration, are two almost meaningless juvenilia by
what I feel were the most gifted poets of my own undergraduate day. The first, from the *Lit* of May 1926, is by
Herman Salinger '27:

A while these futile lips obey,
These heels can feel a bruise,
Whiteness suffuse the brown of clay
And mind pretend to choose.

There will be nothing after this.
The golden bowl will fall apart.
Death will need no artifice
To finger and untie this heart.

The other, from the November *Lit* of the same year, is by A. Y. Fisher '27:

Now the moist roses blow again, and now
The urn of earth is rich with milk and wine,
Now burns the tree like one lamp all aglow,
Shadowing beauty in his face and thine.

Soon comes a bitter season of the year,
Empty the jar, wine-bibber life is gone.
The lamp is lowered by some hand: a flare,
And there are dust and bones in Acheron.

NOTES

1. *Princeton Alumni Weekly,* 21 January 1964.
2. *The New York Review of Books,* preliminary issue.
3. André Malraux, *Les Voix du Silence* (Paris, 1951), p. 333.
4. Unpublished letter quoted in *The Times Literary Supplement,* 28 May 1964, p. 464.
5. Interview in *The New Yorker,* 4 April 1964, p. 35.
6. Malraux, *loc. cit.*

[Prévost d'Exiles, Antoine François]
    Manon Lescaut, 96, 128
Price, George, 148
Propertius, 25, 58, 94, 148
Proust, Marcel, 10, 96
Pythagoras, 30n

[Queneau, Raymond]
    Zazie dans le Métro, 26
Quiller-Couch, Arthur, 172
Quinn, Kenneth, 116n

Racine, Jean Baptiste, 111
Rameau, Jean François, 164
Rand, E. K., 99, 100
Read, Sir Herbert, Knight, 33, 34, 35, 36, 38, 59, 74, 151
Rembrandt, 145
Riese, F. A., 101
Riggs, Thomas, 169
Rivarol, Antoine, 21
Rodd, Hon. Mrs. Peter, 105
Root, R. K., 179n
Rouse, W. H. D., 109, 118n
Rubens, Peter Paul, 145

Saint Paul, 141
Salinger, Herman, 180
Sartre, Jean Paul, 21, 180
Schwartz, Delmore, 130
Scott, Walter, 122
Shakespeare, William, 110
    King Lear, 147
    Romeo and Juliet, 147
    The Tempest, 69
Shattuck, Roger, 37, 115n
Shelley, Percy Bysshe, 10
Snow, C. P., 177
Socrates, 5, 6, 7, 10, 13, 15, 27, 29, 30n, 169
Sophocles, 6, 7, 27, 113, 115n, 121, 143, 148, 150, 159

Antigone, 98
Oedipus Coloneus, 24
Spillane, F. M., 136
Spock, Benjamin, 170
Starkie, W. J., 94
Stein, Gertrude, 42, 79n
Stendhal (Henri Beyle), 96
Stokes, Edward, 31n
Strachey, John St. Loe, 104, 105
Sullivan, J. P., 84, 90, 91, 93, 94, 95, 104, 105, 111, 112
Susemihl, Franz, 166n
Sutherland, Donald, 26, 34, 35, 114, 119n, 165n
Syntopicon, The, 31n

Tartakover, Savielly, 139
Temple, Millie, 40, 56, 58
Tencin, Claudine Alexandrine Guérin de, 29
[Tennyson, Alfred, 1st Baron Tennyson]
    Idylls of the King, 72
Thales, 30n
Thomson, Virgil, 31n
Tillotson, Geoffrey, 107
Tolstoi, Leo N., 10, 18
Trilling, Diana, 133
Turgeniev, Ivan Sergeevich, 77
Turnell, Martin, 31n, 117n
Twain, Mark (Samuel L. Clemens), 46
Tyrrell, Robert Yelverton, 94

Valéry, Paul, 21, 31n
Vergil, 26, 97, 114, 115n, 116n, *Æneid,* 108
Vilmorin, Louise de, 27

Wain, John, 76n, 122, 129
Warman, M. S., 114n
Warren, Robert Penn, 28
Welty, Eudora, 145